THE STRATH: THE BIOGRAPHY OF STRATHPEFFER

THE STRATH

THE BIOGRAPHY OF STRATHPEFFER

SCOTLAND'S FAMOUS SPA, AND DISTRICT

CLARENCE FINLAYSON

FOREWORD BY THE EARL OF CROMARTIE

ETCHINGS BY ALLAN HALDANE

THE SAINT ANDREW PRESS
EDINBURGH

First published in 1979 by The Saint Andrew Press, Edinburgh.

Copyright © J. Clarence Finlayson, 1979

ISBN 0 7152 0432 7

Printed and bound in Great Britain by John G Eccles Printers Ltd, Henderson Road, Inverness.

DEDICATION

*This book is dedicated to my Parents who
brought me up in the Strath, and to my
Wife without whose practical encouragement
it would not have been produced.*

Near here is a valley, birchwoods, heather
and a stream . . . No country, no place was
ever for a moment so delightful to my soul.

Robert Louis Stevenson, *Letters*

Contents

Foreword   9

Introduction   12

1   The Dim and Distant Past   15

2   The Historical Period   31

3   After the 'Forty-Five   53

4   The Spa   71

5   Post-War Years   92

Bibliography   96

List of Illustrations

	Page
The Strath, a general view	Frontispiece
Approaching the summit of Knockfarrel	16
A reconstruction of an early Celtic settlement (BBC copyright photograph)	18
The 'Silly Stones' (By courtesy of the National Monuments Record of Scotland)	20
The Eagle Stone	22
Knockfarrel, from the heights of Achterneed	24
A standing stone, with its mysterious 'cup marks' (By courtesy of the National Monuments Record of Scotland)	26
A crannog on Loch Kinellan	36
Castle Leod	38
Petition to the Court of the Lord Lyon Scotland (By courtesy of THE SCOTSMAN)	43
The largest Spanish chestnut tree in Great Britain	45/46
Monument to the memory of the Honourable Caroline Mackenzie (By courtesy of the National Monuments Record of Scotland)	51
The old mill at Milnain	55
Elsik House	66
The Square, Strathpeffer	72
The Pump Room in the spa season (By courtesy of the National Monuments Record of Scotland)	75
Strathpeffer: a jewel in the Highland casket	77
The old railway station — facing the former site of the Eagle Stone at Tympan Mill — prophesy fulfilled? (By courtesy of the National Monuments Record of Scotland)	79
Ah! the pleasures of a peat bath (By courtesy of the National Monuments Record of Scotland)	81
Firefly: the first aeroplane seen in the Highlands (By courtesy of the Curator, Inverness Museum)	87
The memorial gate of Fodderty churchyard	89
The new Pump Room	94

Foreword

By the Earl of Cromartie

I am delighted to write a short foreward for Clarence Finlayson's *The Strath: the biography of Strathpeffer.* Both of us spent some of the happiest days of our lives in this beautiful place. Indeed, the author, Kenny MacMaster, Mrs Littlejohn (nee MacRae), my late younger brother and I, sat in the same class room in Fodderty school . . . a long time ago.

This book has been a joy to read. It is well researched and gives a vivid and well balanced account of our strath*through the ages.

Pre-history is a difficult subject, and the advent of carbon dating together with the recent finds along the course of the river Danube, especially in Bulgaria, have not only pushed back the dates of many 'finds' of advanced metalurgical craftmanship but also that of stone structures with religious and burial significance, and that of many types of *duns* (forts) as well. The metal work especially is of a very high quality and pre-dates artefacts introduced from the Middle East by way of Egypt. Previously, eminent archeologists calculated their dates from inscriptions written at the time of the first Pharaoh; indeed, there was no other way until carbon dating was developed. This applied also to the British Isles, especially Ireland, and trade between that country and Scotland has existed for thousands of years. Clarence Finlayson gives a clear and exciting picture of these far-off days, well salted with very old legendary stories of the great 'giant heroes' as well as the Fians and fairies of our Highlands.

When we come to historical times written accounts of important events, including battles, are hard to check due often to deliberate destruction, so that we find the interpretation of these happenings vary, depending on the sympathies or interests of the writer. This is particularly true of the eighteenth and nineteenth centuries and, indeed, some twentieth century writers — who were almost invariable Whig in sympathy and violently anti-Highland (of which

*a valley, from the 'srath'.

9

they knew remarkably little). Our author has, of course, avoided this partisan approach and has given a most fair account; but then he is blessed by being a Highlander himself, as well as being a most conscientious scholar.

We discussed together the problem of the Brahan Seer, so beloved by the tourist industry, but there is no trace of this seer in historical ecclesiastical, judicial, or burgh records. But before me as I write I have a copy of one of the Foulis (Munro) Papers which gives the list of the Commissioners selected by the 'Top Brass' in Edinburgh to try one Kenneth Odhar during January 1577-78 for witchcraft etc. Among the many Commissioners appointed is Colin Mackenzie, Chief of Kintail, the grandfather of the First Earl of Seaforth whose first wife was Barbara daughter of John Grant of Grant, (his second wife was Mary, daughter of Mackenzie of Davockmaluag). That great geologist Hugh Miller, the Cromarty stone mason who lived in the early years of the nineteenth century, knew and recorded many of the old Highland stories and he states that the seer Kenneth Odhar — presumably the 'historical' candidate mentioned in the documents of 1577 — was not executed at Fortrose or anywhere else but, though somewhat lacking in his wits, lived to a ripe old age, wandering about the Highlands. But it is a good story and I think that the author has, with a reasonable caveat, dealt with 'the Brahan Seer' very well. It is quite possible that the minister responsible for the book published on this in 1860 collected a great number of prophecies which had been pronounced by many seers of different periods and credited them all to one man who, to say the least, is shadowy.

For those who know and love the Strath and others who will discover it, this book is a must, and if I have been of any help to Clarence Finlayson in this work, I am both proud and happy.

Cromartie

Acknowledgments

Grateful acknowledgment is made to the Royal Commission on the Ancient and Historical Monuments of Scotland for information about the early period in the Strathpeffer region, and for various photographs kindly supplied. I would also like to thank the following for much help in various ways: The Earl and the Countess of Cromartie; Mrs Maureen Cameron; Mr I McCrae; Dr D J Macdonald; Dr Jean Maclennan; Rev I Mactaggart; Rev W Matheson; Mrs E Marshall (Elizabeth Sutherland); Mr E Meldrum; Miss Anne Roska; and Mr K T S Campbell for help in both historical matters and proof corrections.

Introduction

Strathpeffer, at least as far as Scotland is concerned, is unique. Not, of course, in the style of regal Edinburgh, nor yet the smaller but more garish Aviemore, but in its own peculiar fashion. This comes out, for example, in the way local people refer to it. In previous times it was not in order to call it a town, as this term was applicable only to burghs, and the local people, though they talked about the matter, never got around to assuming responsibility for their own management and finance — though now, we notice, since 'burghs' as such no longer exist, the Highlands and Islands Development Board Planning Department do write of Strathpeffer as a town. On the other hand the word 'village' was not used either. Villages did not have 100-bedroom hotels, public gardens and so forth. Reference books delicately avoided the difficulty by writing about it as a health resort, or, more specifically, as the Spa. But for the local people it was normally 'the Strath' — Strath, that is with a capital letter. The valley was a strath (small 's') but we went 'up (or down) the Strath' as others went up town. We preferred not to place our community in any fixed category, leaving it to be assumed that, like Topsy, it had 'just growed'.

This same indeterminateness is also apparent in the very term Strathpeffer Spa — the first part of which suggests Celtic fringe, rather barbaric culture, the second, continental sophistication. Yet all is carried off with admirable aplomb. Visitors find much of the scenery more like Cotswold country than that normally associated with the Scottish Highlands. In many ways it is also border country between Norse and Celt, English and Gael, and bridge country across the centuries. Man has ranged these hills eking out a living, for at least 7000 years, from times when the going was hard indeed, to our own age when in a carpeted, centrally-heated room he may watch in colour a BBC representation of how we today suppose our remote predecessors actually lived. During these centuries culture grew upon culture in rich diversity; to our knowledge dwellers in the strath have spoken at least five different languages.

All things change. Yet the more they change the more they are the same. So, standing on the heights and looking out on the glorious hills, one experiences so great a sense of peace that all the centuries seem to coalesce. One becomes conscious of the underlying unity of all mankind, and the all-embracing Spirit behind Creation.

Ben Wyvis

Most people would expect in any description of Strathpeffer considerable reference to Ben Wyvis (3429 feet above sea level), by far the highest mountain mass on the eastern shores of Great Britain. In this work, however, it has little mention for though the Ben's usual ascent is through Achterneed, the Strath itself is one of the few places for miles around from which it is not visible. The best views are from the Inverness district where it blocks the northern horizon. But the valley of the Peffrey nestles in the folds of its skirts below, and looks not on the face of the great mother that shields it. And shield it she does, her bulk taking the force of the western gales and heavy rain.

The upper reaches of the mountain consist of a series of plateaux of more interest to the botanist than the mountaineer. The way to the top is largely a long, rather tiring walk. But the apparently unexciting large expanses of open territory should not deceive the climber into a false sense of security. The going is treacherous underfoot and mists gather quickly out of what was recently a friendly sky.

Up to the middle of last century the people of the Heights of Achterneed knew every knoll and corrie intimately, and had names for each one. Today they are largely forgotten. Meantime the Ben itself retains its name. What may it have meant to those who first settled this land? Professor W J Watson gives a perfectly simple and straightforward translation of 'Ben Wyvis'. He says it just means 'The High Mountain'. But we prefer the suggestion of other scholars like J B Johnston with overtones of mystery and the supernatural. After all the Bible has its holy mountains; for the Greeks Mount Olympus was the home of the gods, and, while the Brocken has its spectre, the Himalayas are the haunt of the yeti. It would, therefore, be strange if this Highland Ben did not evoke reactions in the minds and emotions of those who lived about it.

From afar it dominated the countryside, ever changing in light and colour — now clear against the sky, again covered with a mantle of snow, and, yet again, invisible as it wrapped its face in the clouds of mist. But to the one who actually scaled its highest reaches it would seem even more august in its isolation. A man assailed by sudden storm upon its summit would feel small indeed! Here was a world too great for him to cope with. He would freely acknowledge powers superior to his own! Yet, on a fine, clear day he might feel even more deeply moved. He would be surveying a scene unsurpassed in our island, covering no fewer than seven modern counties and extending to three oceans: west to the mighty Atlantic, north to the stormy Pentland Firth, east to the North Sea. Over these horizons could lie Ultima Thule, beyond which there was nothing, and Tir-nan-og, the Land of Eternal Youth. Who knows? Surely this must be a seat of the gods themselves.

1.   The Dim and Distant Past

As one motors up the broad, fertile valley of the Peffrey from Dingwall one might be surprised to learn that only a thousand years ago — the time of the Vikings, Macbeth and the Norman Conquest — the road on which we are travelling was deep under the waters of what was then called by the Norse, the Brae Fiord. This extension of the present Cromarty Firth went inland as far as Fodderty Churchyard with swamps and a loch beyond. Indeed, not so long ago on the lands of the present Farm of Brae, just off the northern side of the road, there was unearthed the skeleton of a whale. (This would at the time not be an unwelcome event for the stranding of a whale would be encouraged by local people who would make good use of almost every part of the carcase). Great forests then clothed the hillsides, concealing not only creatures still with us but others long banished from our land, like the wolf, the bison and the bear.

Knockfarrel

But, despite the trees, the queer knob-shaped protuberance ahead must always have been a point of geographical interest. It is now called Knockfarrel. Until early this century there was a good drive along the base of the Cat's Back. Nowadays approach by car must be made from the south side, by Maryburgh, though there are several footpaths from Strathpeffer by which ascent may be made in about half an hour. Knockfarrel is about 800 feet high, but from the top a magnificent view may be had of Ben Wyvis, the Cromarty Firth and the distant mountains of west and south. Today a striking feature, so in the past it must always have been a focal point for races now long forgotten.

Knockfarrel is a very important feature in the district, being one of the best examples we have of a vitrified fort. It was excavated in the 1770's by John Williams who published his results, so producing one of the first scientific works of the kind. Little has been done on

15

Approaching Summit of Knockfarrel from Strathpeffer

Allan Haldane.

the site since. The area of the fort was 425 feet by 125 feet, with the walls from 8 to 15 feet high, and outlying projections. The stones were interlaced with a wooden framework which at some time was ignited, such heat being generated thereby that the stones were welded together. This was probably caused either by enemy action or the accidental ignition of the lean-to huts situated against the inside walls.

The question thus arises as to who raised the fort and when. Isabel Henderson in her book *The Picts* notes that Knockfarrel is one of the most northerly vitrified forts in Scotland, just south of the area of the brochs which cluster densely in eastern Sutherland and Caithness. She maintains that this is an outlier of one of the two northern settlements of Celtic refugees from the Roman conquests in the south. Since then, however, Craig Phadrig, above Inverness, has been excavated and tests establish that it was erected pre-500 BC, several centuries before the Celts arrived.

Since both forts seem to belong to a group with a third at North Kessock, it would seem likely that Knockfarrel too was built by a race antecedent to even the Celts. Such undertakings, says Edward Meldrum, required an immense force for their construction, and indicate a considerable population. He also maintains that they were the product of an heroic age like those of Greece and Rome on the continent of Europe. Times had become so relatively secure and comfortable that each clan had a group of warriors for whom fighting was a way of life. Perhaps modern sporting contests are not so very different in essence. But, if life was more exciting, it was also more dangerous, and these strongholds had to be built on points of vantage for the protection of the tribe and their stock. They also served as bases from which they could command the countryside, exacting tolls from passing travellers and traders. But, of course, for the ordinary people life proceeded along much more prosaic lines as Alexander the Great realised, more or less in that age, when he noted that the peasants of India continued their ploughing unconcernedly while world-changing battles were taking place all around them.

If the date pre-500 is confirmed, it brings us near 753 BC, the traditional date for the founding of Rome, also upon hills. One wonders to what extent it is a coincidence that these early ancestors of ours were also reputed to have been small and dark; possibly Mediterranean types? Certain features in their culture, including building techniques, also bear similarity.

In 1978 the BBC produced a series of television programmes showing a group of young people living in a comparable environment in the south of England, simulating as far as they could the life of a small community of Celts in about 300 BC. Superficially, at least, there was a great deal of likeness between the two settlements. In both there were small circular huts and lean-tos against the inside of a surrounding wall, and a larger house in the centre. In the televised experiment the latter was a communal dwelling, but it has been conjectured that the corresponding feature on Knockfarrel might have been the house of the chief.

There remain many things about Knockfarrel awaiting excavation, and, with virtually nothing along this line having been undertaken since John Williams's time, it is possible that an enterprising modern archaeologist could still make exciting discoveries.

The First Inhabitants

But, though the age of the vitrified forts takes us back to some time near the founding of the city of Rome it is sobering to think that men had been living on the hills round about for a much longer period prior to this time than since then to the present day. Traces have been left by little groups of wandering hunters who ranged the countryside as early as 5000 BC. Within the next 2000 years, however, their numbers increased, and they settled down to practise the art of farming. Primitive they may have been in some ways, but we should not underestimate either their intelligence or their technical skill. They had a strong social sense, and meditated much on the meaning of life and death. Sometimes they favoured inhumation, sometimes cremation. Above Jamestown there is a 'barrow' grave. Some 'henges' (so called after Stonehenge) in the Strathpeffer district are so unclear that archaeologists have wondered if these earthworks represent a pre-henge stage of development laid out before 2000 BC. There is a double circle of smallish stones on the summit of the Cat's Back, but high above Fodderty on the boundary with Tulloch estate there is a similar circle of large stones, most of them now spread-eagled on the ground. To the Gaels of the tenth century AD they were more of a mystery than to us, for they called them, in Gaelic, the 'Silly Stones'. But the most impressive relics of all are the two great monoliths at Inchvannie, in the grounds of the house which was once the parish church and which stands next to Fodderty School. These bear on them the curious cup-marks which are found elsewhere but the significance of which is unknown. Local legends have

grown up round these stones as we relate elsewhere (Page 25).

The Celts and the Picts

The Celts were a people who began to settle in Britain in the two centuries or so before the time of Christ. They originated in Central Europe, went east as far as the New Testament Galatia in Asia Minor, south through Italy and west to the Atlantic. Their influence remains to this day in our place-names. London received its name from them and we may compare the Italian 'Apennines' with the English 'Pennines'. Reaching the Strath the Celts liked our local stream and called it the 'Peffrey' or 'Sparkler' (forms of the same river name can be traced in Cheshire (the Peover) and in Italy (the Piferari), Within the first few centuries of the Christian era, however, Brythonic, their particular Celtic dialect, disappeared from our island except from Wales, where, in its modern form, it is still the beloved tongue of its people. Elsewhere it succumbed to English and to Gaelic spoken by a related Celtic tribe, the Gaels, who came from Spain, took over Ireland and gradually spread into the Isle of Man and Western and Northern Scotland.

The Picts, however are a different matter. Who precisely they were and what language they spoke, has for centuries been a matter of dispute among scholars. Sir Walter Scott has his Antiquary engaged in a fierce wrangle on the point, and today the argument still continues. We know they had their own language but there is difference of opinion as to whether it was merely a form of Celtic or completely non-Aryan. Dr W F H Nicolaison cuts the Gordian Knot by suggesting they they had two languages, which is not unlikely when we consider the background. When waves of newcomers arrived they seem to have been assimilated comparatively peacefully, and the invading Celts (Brythonic in this case) did not find inferior savages but a people with a well-developed culture, with much to give as well as to receive. Stray examples of their speech have been recorded as inscriptions on stone and in one case (a king-list) on vellum, but though the letters are clear enough, the language is completely indecipherable (for example, 'ettocuhetts ahehhttannn hocvvevv nehhtons'!). The main guide we have is that Pictish place-names often begin with 'Pit-' (eg Pitglassie, a farm to the south east of Knockfarrel). No fewer than 300 names with the prefix 'Pit-' have been listed, nearly all in eastern Scotland.

Of course every schoolboy knows that Julius Caesar called these people 'Picti' because they painted their naked bodies with woad to

Allan Haldane

Eagle Stone, Strathpeffer.

terrify their enemies, but the application of this piece of information to Northern Scotland is of doubtful value. (We are told that this happened to be one of the cold, wet periods of our British climate and one supposes that pneumonia was as likely then as now!) What is of importance for our study is that the Picts left all over the North-East the finest and most impressive examples of a native art to have survived the Dark Ages, their fantastic and beautiful stone-carvings. Two good examples in the neighbourhood are the Eagle Stone (Clach an Tiompan) in Strathpeffer itself and the symbol-stone just inside the gate of the Churchyard in Dingwall.

The Eagle Stone

The Eagle Stone, now standing in the field off Nutwood Lane, has two typically Pictish symbols skilfully incised upon its surface: at the top an arch or horseshoe shape ornamented with curved lines and small circles, and beneath, the characteristic Pictish bird, carved with great dignity and power. This stone, of the Class I variety (Romilly Allan), could possibly be dated 650 to 750 AD. The Dingwall stone though in a much poorer condition, has even more of the typically Pictish signs upon it. The meaning of these symbol stones is quite obscure but several stories and theories of very doubtful authenticity have grown up (See page 19). Under Pictish law, succession appears usually to have gone through the female line (a relic of the way of life of the very early races?), and this could lead to complicated situations, making fixed boundary marks very useful. One interesting suggestion is that the Eagle Stone is a marriage stone. The upper symbol, the horseshoe, would signify the dominant family.

It is also just possible that the horseshoe could be a symbol of femininity, signifying the bride's family.

Dr Henderson confesses that she is tempted to associate the dissemination of the symbolism with King Brude who received St Columba in his royal fortress in Inverness. The location of the stones throughout Pictland speaks of a settled community, and the great expertise of the carvings a concern for culture which is impressive. The later development in Christian forms as Classes II and III may have been the special preserve of certain families — a very fine type of the later 'travelling people' — who handed down their skills to succeeding generations.

The coming of the Gaels we have already mentioned, but they did not reach the north-east till after their union with the Picts under

Kenneth MacAlpine about 841 AD. The details of what happened are by no means clear but with the Norsemen now pressing in from the north the Picts seem suddenly to have allowed themselves to be assimilated by the Gaels encroaching from the south. As a result the old Pictish traditions and other ways of life, together with their distinctive language, disappeared. From then onward mainstream culture in Northern Scotland became decisively Gaelic-speaking except where the Norse had established themselves.

Tales of Finn mac Coul

The old fort on the hill above the Strath the newcomers called Knockfarrel ('the hill of the high, projecting stone house'). Considering how there must still have been in the minds of the Picts some recollection of how much it had meant in the history of their own people, it is surprising that they let go forever the name by which they and their ancestors had known it. But Gaelic has always been a rich source of folk tales, of legends, of heroic deeds. Perhaps, indeed, there was a mingling of the two traditions. In any case it was not long before the sennachie at the ceilidh and the mother telling her bed-time story, were using the local scene as a setting for the stories of long ago.

The Great Hero of the Gaels was Finn mac Coul, Fingal of the tales of Ossian. That the old fort would provide a suitable abode for mac Coul's heroic companions was obvious, and fertile imaginations would use other local features in adapting old tales and inventing new ones. For instance, the great standing stones in the valley had to be explained. So stories readily came to lips of how the ancient warriors used to engage in trials of strength, tossing rocks over the Strath. But even in those days it sometimes happened that the weather spoiled people's sport, and when the footholds were slippery the stones, instead of clearing the valley, landed deep in the hollow. Look, there are the finger-and-thumb marks of the giants on that stone to this day!

What of the signs of burning on the fort walls? From these arose the tale of how the giants went a-hunting to Nigg accompanied by their dogs, of which Finn's favourites were Bran and Sgeolan (pronounced Scolaing). Garry, a dwarf (only 15 feet tall), was left in charge at the fort, much to his annoyance. He gave vent to his displeasure by storming at the women, and then, going outside, stretched himself on the grass and fell asleep. The women took

advantage of the opportunity to peg the plaits of his hair to the ground so effectively that when Garry awoke he nearly scalped himself in trying to pull himself free. Now in a furious temper, he barricaded the women and children indoors and burned the fortress down. From afar the warriors saw the blaze and vaulted home on their spears. They caught the fleeing Garry and offered him the choice of death. The vindictive dwarf-giant chose beheading with his neck on Finn's knees. Needless to say the ensuing blow not only killed Garry but mortally wounded Finn. So the desolate giants, bereft of wives, offspring and leader, realised that their rule had come to an end and decided to depart. Bearing the body of the mighty Finn to the Craigiehowe Cave at the mouth of Munlochy Bay, they entered, laid down their burden reverently, arranged themselves around and fell asleep . . .

Centuries passed. Then one day a shepherd chanced on the cave and, going inside, saw before him the giants and their hounds stretched out in all their barbaric grandeur. Above the door there hung a hunting horn which he tentatively took down and put to his lips. As he blew he noted with alarm that the giants' eyes were now open but as otherwise they did not stir he risked a second blast upon the horn. With this the giants sat up resting on their left elbows. Unnerved, the shepherd fled with the anguished cry of the only half-liberated sleepers ringing in his ears: *'Dhuine dhon dh'fhag thu sinn na's moisa na fhuair thu sinn.'* ('Wretch, you have left us worse than you found us!') An interesting feature of this tale is that while in Irish legend Finn's life is terminated at the ford of Brea (Bray), in the Highland Scottish version this event takes place on the hill above the Brae Fiord or, as it is now known, the Cromarty Firth.

The Vikings

Hardly, however, had the Gaels established their mastery over the Strath when from the hills they would have seen the square-sailed boats in the Firth below: to their shores had come the Norsemen from whose fury monks further south prayed fervently to be delivered. Not that the event was unexpected, for the Vikings had long since established themselves in the far north, and gradually extended their control southward. In this situation Dingwall Castle was a key-point for the whole of the north of Scotland, and in one of our most ancient maps, that of Matthew Paris (died 1259), while there is no note of Inverness, 'Castrum Dinkeual' (Dingwall Castle) is given equal prominence with 'Edeneburg' and 'Glascu'. When Picts and Scots were united under Kenneth MacAlpine, Scotland was divided into nine districts, of which Ross was one. Ross and Moray were ruled by a 'mormaer' (steward of the sea) of royal blood.

In the years immediately after 1000 AD, Dingwall (then called Inverpeffrey), was held by a mormaer named Finlay. He himself was murdered, and succeeded by his son Macbeth — none other than the famous character of Shakespeare's play, who was probably born and reared in Dingwall though he spent little of his mature life there.

We are here in a period of history where information is sparse and confusing, and it must be said Shakespeare, who is so notoriously careless about geography and dates, does not help. The play opens with a battle which may be an echo of the notable Battle of Torfness between Thorfinn the Norseman and a Scottish King often identified by historians as King Duncan. However, our local historians prefer to argue that this was Duncan's grandfather, Malcolm II. The Orknewinga Saga gives the Viking version:

> The wolf's bit (= sword) reddened its edge
> In the place called Torfness.
> A young ruler (= Thorfinn) caused it.
> This happened on a Monday.
> In the conflict south of Ekkial
> The thin (sharpened) swords sang
> When the gallant Prince fought
> With the King of Scotland.

Since the battle took place south of Ekkial (Oykel) some historians have located it on the shores of the Breda Fiord which is the Moray Firth. They are probably unaware that the nearer Firth, the Cromarty Firth, had at that time an extension, called by the Norse the Brae Fiord which went up what is now the Strathpeffer valley past what is to this very day Brae Farm. Since there are almost no traces of Norse influence in Morayshire and so much from the River Beauly north, the Ross-shire site is surely to be preferred. With this presumption the Tor is very obviously Knockfarrel. Furthermore, say local historians, most of the fighting took place on the ridge still called Coil-an-righ. Here Malcolm was seriously wounded and carried from the battle on the long journey to Glamis Castle where he died.

Malcolm was succeeded by his grandson King Duncan of the play. He and Thorfinn were cousins, but they were far from being friends and the Norseman continuing to decline to pay tribute, the King marched north to enforce his will. He was met near Elgin by a coalition between Thorfinn and Macbeth where he was defeated and killed. Macbeth at this opportunity seized the throne making as it turned out an excellent ruler, leaving Thorfinn to his own devices.

In any case there is no doubt that for a century Dingwall was a Norse stronghold. Thorfinn, in undisputed control, ruled from the castle for the rest of his days, setting up his *Thingvollr* (parliament) on the mound behind Mill Street, which may still be inspected. *Thingvollr* is, of course, the origin of the name of the modern town Dingwall.*

The Norse Occupation

Having arrived and conquered, the invaders soon pressed on inland in the direction of the Strath. At their head wad Jarl Olaf, who also probably built himself a castle on the site where Castle Leod now stands. Of noble blood, probably a relative of Thorfinn, he seems to have been a strong personality. To this day the hill behind his house is called Knockowlah — Olaf's Hill — suggesting that it must have been the scene of many hunting and other memorable adventures. Westward, he had his farm spreading up the valley over the present golf-course, Ulladale — Olaf's Dale.

His followers also had their choice of land. They liked what they saw and sent back to their homeland for their families. The latter may have been reluctant to leave their homes and make the dangerous crossing of the North Sea, but no doubt once they had settled in they would realise what a good exchange they had made. No longer an impoverished peasantry, scraping a living out of unwilling soil, they had now become the aristocracy among Gaelic natives compelled to do their bidding.

They pushed on past Ulladale, leaving a settlement at Kinellan, but they did not touch the Coul estate, then a marsh. On higher levels they reached the Blackwater River with its falls, which they called 'Rogie' ('splashing'), and viewed the leaping salmon not with the tourist's present-day eye but as a tasty item for supper. The invaders, however, do not seem to have settled at Rogie. Leastwise, the Vikings were traditionally tall, and there is a local proverb

*The official Gaelic title of the town is, as we have said, Inverpeffrey. The friendly designation used frequently today even by non-Gaelic speakers is Bailechaul — Cabbage-Town!

which mocks at Rogie people as unusually diminutive. It is just possible that here was a pocket of people descended with unmixed blood from the original inhabitants of the land, supposed to be small and swarthy, with Mediterranean characteristics. In any case, the Norsemen swept on past Contin and Achilty and established a tax-centre at Scatwell where the Gaels had to pay taxes for the land which had once been their own.

Ardguie

The biggest single settlement of invaders was probably at the eastern end of Strathpeffer at the top of the Nutwood Lane. It was called Ardguie and was marked on local maps until the end of the eighteenth century when the development of the later Spa caused the site to be merged in modern building. The name, which it would surely be good to preserve, means 'the height of the Danes'.

This suggests there were two strains in the invading force: the majority, referred to as *Gall,* being from Norway, and the minority, *Guie* or *Ghuile* from Denmark (possibly connected with the modern Danish name for Jutland, 'Jylland'). Dingwall also had one or two settlements of the latter.

The Norse dominance, however, did not last much more than a century, for in numbers they were much inferior to the Gaels among whom they had settled.

For a generation or two the Norse community remained separate and dominant; then, through social contact and inter-marriage, their language, customs and separate identity gradually merged with those of the surrounding population, so that the memory of the Viking invasion was quite lost, except in a few place-names.

Yet perhaps in a subtle way their influence still lives on, for in the Highland area there are two distinct strains of people. This may be seen in various contexts, including the churches they attend. But it is most easily identifiable when we compare the types of folk on the western and eastern seaboards respectively. To this day the former tends to be introspective, emotional, rich in music and poetry, while the latter are now extrovert and practical. The easterner has no songs of his own, nor is he very worried about the lack. Strangely enough both types are mixtures of Gael and Norseman, so that their different outlooks must be due to tradition rather than blood.

2. The Historical Period

We now pass from the time of few written records and many foreign invasions to one where we can be more precise and where unrest is the result of internal strife.

Snapshot of the Past

In the Middle Ages the main settlement in the Strath was Ardguie where there was, until two centuries ago, a group of cottages with outhouses. Isolated dwellings were not very popular in a rough age; it was a matter of prudence to dwell in a community for protection against the depredations of stray marauders or hostile clansmen. Throughout the Highlands, much land remained in common use and ownership, and people co-operated in cutting peats and herding and tending cattle. The community spirit being so strong, doors were kept unbarred — at least in times of peace — and in the long dark evenings of winter neighbours gathered around the cottage fire to exchange song and story.

From Ardguie looking north and west, the hillside in harvest was covered with strips of golden grain, right up to the present church-yard at Kinnettas which then possessed not only the burial ground but a long, low church with a thatched roof. Skirting the graveyard was a drove road which at the junction with a farm track had a well, used alike by residents and passers-by. A pump which supplanted the well was still in use until just before the First World War. In the valley below ran the burn till it reached the end of Ardival Road where it was dammed to make a farm pond. From this it tumbled downward to work the wheel of Ardival Mill which still stood at the bottom of the garden of what was the original farmhouse.

No longer the farmhouse (which is now higher up the hill), Ardival House is the oldest house in the area and possesses many interesting features. It is reputed at one time to have been an inn; with its one external door on to the road at the higher level in addition to three on the lower, it would be well adapted for such a purpose.

The mill itself was not generally known as Ardival Mill but, from the fifteenth century, as the Tympan Mill. Beside the Tympan Mill was originally located the Eagle Stone, known in Gaelic as Clachan-Tiompan, which we have already discussed as a work of art from Pictish days. Before its nature was understood, the stone was thought to have marked the site of an encounter in 1411 between the army of the Lord of the Isles and the defenders of the Earldom of Ross. Donald, Lord of the Isles, had marched with a very large force to do battle for lands in Aberdeenshire which he thought were part of his rightful inheritance. It was a time of great turmoil in Scottish history, and some have maintained that on the outcome of the conflict depended the very succession to the throne. In any case, the Lord of the Isles was determined to assert *en passant* the validity of his claim to the Earldom of Ross, whose official incumbent was abroad. The Regent Albany had put Dingwall Castle in the hands of Angus Dubh MacKay of Farr. MacKay gathered a force of clansmen, mainly Munros, and met the opposing host in the valley where Strathpeffer now stands. The battle was fierce, MacKay being killed and his brother captured; still, in spite of their misfortune, it was enough to halt the Lord of the Isles in his progress. Instead of continuing down the Strath towards Dingwall, he turned south over Knockfarrel and so to Inverness. Many Munros were killed, and since the crest of the Munros includes the head of an eagle, some thought that the Eagle Stone had been set up in commemoration of their heroic deaths.

The Coming of the Mackenzies

During the fifteenth century Ross witnessed the rise of one dominant family, the Mackenzies, who have been intimately connected with Strathpeffer down to the present day. The ancient Earldom of Ross was to all intents and purposes extinct by the late 1400's; the MacDonalds had played the power game unsuccessfully, and the title had been taken back by the Crown. The power vacuum was filled by the Mackenzies, whose inveterate hostility to the Lords of the Isles stood them in good stead.

It is strange that many of our most famous Scottish names (e.g. Fraser, Bruce, Gordon) are not Scottish in origin but were introduced to this country by Norman followers of feudal monarchs. Not so the Mackenzies, who are of pure Celtic stock. They themselves trace their origin to a certain Kenneth living in 1267 at

Eilean Donan, an island stronghold at the mouth of Loch Duich which eats into the mountains of Kintail opposite the southern end of Skye. Actually the roots of this family may go back some generations further. There is a well-founded tradition that as early as the 1100's when the Lords of the Isles held sway not only down the west coast of Scotland but as far as Dublin, the Scottish King, William the Lion, gave a Kintail progenitor of the family a financial grant to curb as far as he could this menace to the royal authority. In the course of the centuries the threat passed from the hands of the Norse aliens to the native MacDonalds, but, through it all, the Mackenzies kept up a constant and in the end victorious rivalry with the Island power.

During this age-long vendetta the Crown and the Mackenzies maintained an occasionally rather tenuous friendship. The tradition of unswerving loyalty on the part of the clan is not entirely borne out by the facts, but it is encouraged by various stories, such as how Kenneth of Kintail saved the King from the charge of a wounded stag.

As his arrow sped to its target he shouted, 'Cuidich an Righ! Cuidich an Righ!' ('Save the King! Save the King!') To this heroic rescue is attributed the royal authorisation of the deer's antlers in the Mackenzie coat-of-arms. Some authorities, claim that 'Cuidich an Righ' only means 'Tribute to the King'. The tradition of the rescue, however, is stoutly maintained in Mackenzie country to this day; hence the large numbers of houses, hotels and clubs (including, of course, the Strathpeffer Shinty Team) who dignify their titles by the inclusion of the word 'Caberfeidh' (Antlers). Similarly current is a story that Mackenzie of Kintail sheltered Robert Bruce in 1306 when he was in hiding from his enemies, in spite of the hostility of neighbouring chiefs.

Blar-na-Pairc or The Battle of Park
However the Mackenzies were usually more interested in local rather than national affairs, and were constantly asserting themselves as the greatest clan in the north of Scotland. One story concerns a fight with the expressive title of Blar-nan-Ceann or the Battle of the Heads which took place at Park, in the area roughly where the youth hostel now stands, and between Kinellan and the Cat's Back in 1487.

The antagonist was, of course, the Lord of the Isles, a female relative of whom had been married to the Mackenzie heir to improve his clan's standing. The Lady Margaret, however, as well as a biting tongue, possessed only one eye and Mackenzie determined to send her back to the Isles mounted on a one-eyed horse, accompanied by a one-eyed servant and followed by a one-eyed dog. Lady Margaret's brother did not enjoy the joke, nor was he mollified on hearing that Mackenzie had already remarried, this time a Miss Fraser of Lovat.

Retaliation, which could not have been unexpected, was swift. The MacDonalds, led by Gillespie, cousin of the Lord of the Isles, swept down upon the village of Contin to find that the able-bodied men of the district had withdrawn to prepare for battle but that the women, children and infirm had gathered in the church for sanctuary. Gillespie showed no mercy, stacking piles of wood round the building and setting all alight. Distantly, from the heights around, spectators watched the proceedings over the next two hours as the church was gradually burned to the ground, but MacDonald remained unmoved. It may have been that he hoped the Mackenzie force would risk an assault to save their families; if they had come down he would have been able to destroy them, but if this was in his mind the ruse did not succeed.*

When the battle took place, it was bitter indeed. The Mackenzies were assisted by several of the clan Brodie, but their numbers were much inferior to their opponents. Nonetheless they fought with such determination that they completely overwhelmed the invaders in the general area of where Jamestown now stands. Such of the latter as escaped fled over the Bealach (pass) down to the fast flowing River Conon at Moy, where they enquired of a local woman how best to get across.

(It is strange how few Highlanders are able to swim, despite the fact that they never live far from the sea, loch or stream.) The lady had herself suffered from their brutality and no doubt had lost friends in the church fire. So she told them the river was much shallower than it looked, especially in the darker parts. Once most of her enemies were committed to the water, she and her neighbours set about cutting away overhanging branches by which they might reach dry land again. It was reckoned that at least a

*Since circumstantial evidence supports the truth of this cruel episode, one accepts its authenticity. War has many such crimes. But we have to beware of invention and careless reporting, for the same story has been attached to several other churches where it did not happen at all. Similarly, Scott in his *Lord of the Isles* describes how several hundred MacDonalds were suffocated by the MacLeods in a cave on the Island of Eigg. Recent research suggests that this story, once universally accepted, has no basis in fact.

thousand warriors perished that day either in battle or by drowning.

So unlikely was the victory of the Mackenzies against the vast array of the MacDonalds, that it was rumoured that they had had supernatural, if grudging, assistance in the shape of a little man in a red nightcap who appeared suddenly among them. He selected one MacDonald and slew him on the spot, sat down on the body and folded his arms. The Mackenzies naturally asked him why he had suspended operations, whereupon he explained that he had only been paid for one MacDonald. The Mackenzies told him that if he killed another he would be paid double. So he arose, slew another MacDonald, and once again seated himself on the corpse. The Mackenzie chief, being told of this, came running, and said to the grim little man, 'Don't reckon with me, and I'll not stint thee!' Immediately the little man got up and with every blow killed a MacDonald, always saying, 'If you don't trifle with me, I won't trifle with you!' When the battle was over the Mackenzies had won a decisive victory, and many MacDonalds had lost their heads, Gillespie's rolling down into a well where it was found later.* As for the little man, he leapt into the waters of Loch Kinellan, never to be seen again, and apparently without claiming his reward.

There is, however, a historical fact behind the strange tale. Duncan Macrae, aged 19, from Kintail was a huge, ungainly fellow who had drifted towards the battlefield but was disregarded by the warriors. He picked up an old battle-axe but in the conflict did little to aid the Mackenzies amongst whom he found himself. When asked why he did not fight he said 'Unless I get a man's recognition I will not do a man's work'. Promised this, he laid about him with deadly effect, every now and again pausing and sitting down on his last MacDonald victim until he was promised an additional reward. It was his intervention which did much to give the Mackenzies their decisive victory. He did not jump into Loch Kinellan at the end of the day, but retired to Kintail and Gairloch where he did many other deeds of valour, though he was known to the end of his life as Big Duncan of the Axe.

In fact the victory of the Mackenzies was probably due to their superior strategic skill. For their stand they chose a site between which and the MacDonalds there lay an innocent-looking stretch of smooth greensward; this was really a deep quagmire and, charging

*A significant detail which may indicate a submerged myth in this odd story; wells and severed heads are associated in some parts of the Highlands.

a Camping in Loch Kinellan; Strathpeffer.
Oban, Hallows.

across it, the MacDonalds became hopelessly bogged. The Mackenzies appeared from concealed positions and picked them off at their leisure.

Had the MacDonald triumphed on that day, he might well have regained the Earldom of Ross. As it was, the Lordship of the Isles for good or bad fell away and withered from then onwards and the Mackenzies went from strength to strength.

As has already been indicated, in the fifteenth century the chief of the time moved his seat from Eilean Donan to Easter Ross, in fact to Kinellan at the west end of Strathpeffer. Times being unsettled, he decided to build himself a crannog. The idea was nothing new. A crannog was a form of defence common in Western Europe long before the Christian era. If nature did not already provide one, an 'island' was constructed by the transport of large quantities of stones and other debris to a suitable spot. When this was firmed up wooden stakes, usually of oak, were driven in and the fortress given a secure base. The surrounding area was thereupon flooded to the appropriate depth by the damming of an adjacent stream, leaving above water level a jetty for the boat, and at about water level a twisting causeway to the shore, on which in the event of sudden attack the invader would be at an obvious disadvantage. About the time of the First World War the site was fully excavated by Hugh Fraser, science master at Dingwall Academy. Certain finds were made, including a wooden boat in poor condition, which had been used in constructing the foundations. The loch is easily approached either from the golf-course or by the farm road opposite the youth hostel.

The Kinellan crannog was in use for several generations and was the centre of many stirring, often tragic events. In time, however, those who had the means began to aspire to more commodious and comfortable quarters. So Lord Seaforth, as the Kinellan Mackenzie then was, built himself the really palatial castle at Brahan which we shall be describing in detail later. He had, however, just settled into his new abode when he heard that tax commissioners were on their way from Edinburgh to assess him. At once the noble lord pulled up his new roots and returned to Kinellan until the visitors had departed!

The Tutor of Kintail

The sixteenth century progressed; the Mackenzies settled down all over Easter Ross and became extremely ramified, building up what was virtually a small independent kingdom, stretching right across

Allan Haldane.

Castle Leod, Strathpeffer

Scotland from the Black Isle to Lewis. One of the most energetic chieftains of the time, Roderick Mackenzie of Coigach, the Tutor of Kintail, came into possession of Castle Leod near Strathpeffer in 1572, improving it extensively.

It is interesting to note that the name of his residence really has nothing to do with the word 'castle' nor with the MacLeods, though Roderick married a MacLeod. In 1669 we find the Laird of Applecross writing that 'Sir Rorie (Roderick) died at his own house at Culta-Leod in September 1626 being very much regretted by all his countrymen.' Professor Watson thinks the original title may have been 'Cul da Leothad', which means 'At the back of the two slopes', a good description of the castle's location.

Sir Rorie, a forceful character, was known as the Tutor of Kintail because he administered the considerable Kintail estates on behalf of his nephew Colin, later the first Lord Seaforth, who was only eleven when his father died. The estates were at the time in great confusion, but the Tutor dealt with these and his own affairs with insight and efficiency. Out of disorder and rivalry he brought co-operation and peace, occasionally with great firmness. Some of the tenants circulated the saying that the three things most to be dreaded were frost in May, mist in the dog-days, and the Tutor of Kintail!

This firmness is reflected in his management of what may be termed 'foreign affairs'. It was Sir Rorie who really completed the dismemberment of the now moribund Lordship of the Isles, acting with typical Mackenzie decisiveness in 1611 and again in 1622, succeeding where the Crown had failed.*

The Crown acquiesced in this conquest, but how far the Tutor of Kintail was from being uniformly loyal may be seen in the astonishingly heavy fine (£4,000) imposed upon him also in 1611 for giving shelter to members of the proscribed Clan MacGregor, an offence tantamount to treason. The King's writ did not run very far in Ross in those days, and the only real authority was that of the Mackenzie, whose clansmen were in every position of power.

Possessing such patronage, then, many of the Mackenzies at the beginning of the 1600's appear to have become ministers of religion, a position which does not always seem to have restrained their more

---

*The King had earlier attempted to set up a 'plantation' in the Isles on the lines of the more successful venture in Ulster. When the Fife Adventurers (as those involved were styled) burnt their fingers, the Mackenzies bought up their rights. Sir Rorie's actions confirmed these by force of arms.

human impulses. We read of one Mr John Mackenzie, minister of Dingwall, who had in fact also been fined heavily along with Sir Rorie for the same offence in 1611, and who in 1615:

> out of hatred to (George Graham of Drynie) and without respect to the Godlie, honest and peaceable behaviour which beseemeth ane of his calling and professioun, did on the 26th of August send his tenant . . . armed with a long musket charged with many bullets, to wait at ane hous end, behind ane dyke of devotis within the said George's awin toun of Drynie, to attack the said laird . . .
>
> (Bain, *History of Ross* (1899) p. 172)

When Graham appeared, the assassin

> dischargit the musket at him, and lodged seven pellets in his body, five of which still remain there . . . and came runnand upoun him, and with the musket clubbed the said George and left him for dead. Immediately thereafter (further accomplices), persaving the said George going away on his awn feet, they being bodin in feir or weir, with durkis, swordis, targes and pistoletis on their body, followed the said George with all their speed, and . . . schott and dischargit ane pistol at him, and he narrowly escaped with his lyfe.
>
> (Bain, *loc cit*)

Such goings-on appear to have been fairly normal in the Ross of William Shakespeare's time and illustrate the high-handedness with which the chiefs and their kin behaved, as well as the fierce loyalty of their tenants and other followers. It has been said that it must have resembled the Old West of the nineteenth century America, with an over-simmering state of range warfare. But, indeed, is not the modern parallel the football world with competing teams supported by hot-headed passionately loyal young 'fans'? On the other hand, let us also remember it does not represent the whole community. The more sober element largely disregard it and get on with the business of earning a living and the other problems of everyday life. However, the Mackenzies of those times worked their way to the top of the Ross-shire League and there remained, paying not much attention even to the laws from Edinburgh, or, later, London.

Sir Rorie Mackenzie married Margaret, eldest daughter of

40

Torquil MacLeod of Lewis, by which event lands and the name came into the family which a grandson was to make use of in future years. In the meantime their son John, the eldest, obtained a baronetcy of Nova Scotia, a money-making device like the baronetcies of Ulster above referred to, which Charles I, in great financial straits, invented for sale to interested parties.

The Earls of Cromartie

John's son George (1630-1714) followed a political career from the time of Charles II to that of Queen Anne. Employed on one occasion to treat with the clans he did so with such prudence as helped materially to a settlement. He was created Lord Tarbat, and, many years later, the Earl of Cromartie. He had many sides to his character, writing not only a history of the Mackenzies but also expositions of the prophecies of Daniel and St John. Bishop Burnet, William of Orange's adviser on Scottish affairs, remarked of him that he had great notions of religion and virtue, but they were only notions! He was a leading advocate of the union of the two Parliaments in 1707.*

The First Earl of Cromartie is also of some importance in this history because he secured government recognition of the amalgamation of his fourteen far-scattered estates into the County of Cromarty which, united with Ross, gave us the County (now District) of Ross and Cromarty.

He was buried in the ground adjacent to Dingwall Parish Church, and the event was marked by considerable ceremonial. It was said that a domestic servant who bore him a grudge had threatened to desecrate his grave. Whether as a consequence of this or not, tenants from his numerous estates were each instructed to bring a basket of earth which they heaped over the grave creating a considerable mound. On the top of this was erected an obelisk sixty-five feet high which in time developed so serious a tilt that by 1921 it was no less than five feet off the plumb. The Countess of Cromartie then had it taken down, and a smaller replica erected which visitors may see at the foot of Church Street.

Mackenzie loyalty to the Crown continued during the seventeenth-century troubles. They supported Montrose, and were a serious source of trouble to Cromwell. On one occasion the

*It is of interest that the present Earl, the fourth, has been taking a major part in the House of Lords debate on the Devolution Bill (1978).

Presbytery of Dingwall put the clan under discipline. They fought for Charles II at Worcester when many were killed and others sent overseas as slaves. With the Restoration of course the tide turned, and things went well for a period, but when William of Orange succeeded, Seaforth was suspected and was sent to prison for seven years.

The Seaforths thus learnt their lesson and when in 1745 their relative, the Reverend Colin Mackenzie, minister of Fodderty, a strong anti-Jacobite, suddenly appeared at Brahan Castle with news of the landing of Prince Charles in Morar, they were persuaded by him not to join the rising. Instead, with the Reverend Colin they rode hastily to the West Coast to meet fellow clansmen who had just landed from Lewis, and succeeded in persuading them also to return home peaceably.

Not so, however, with the Cromarties; the Earl and his son, Lord MacLeod, raised a considerable force for the Prince's cause. They were, however, eventually defeated at Dunrobin on the day before the Battle of Culloden. Cromartie and his son were both captured and the father was imprisoned with two other Scottish Lords, Kilmarnock and Balmerino, in the Tower of London.

Their trial took place in Westminster Hall, which had been specially fitted out for the occasion. Not only were their peers, as judges, present, but most of London society, including the Prince and Princess of Wales. The three prisoners received the death sentence, but in the case of Lord Cromartie it was not carried out. As the King was one day entering the Royal Chapel at Kensington Palace, the Countess of Cromartie with her ten children (and another's arrival imminent) suddenly appeared.

She fell on her knees clutching the royal coat-tails, presented a petition for her husband's life, and fainted. So a reprieve was granted on condition that the prisoner never returned to Scotland. The title was attainted, the lands forfeited and the castle for a time garrisoned.

The royal clemency was appreciated by the Earl's son, Lord MacLeod who, after service with the King of Sweden, returned to this country and received approval for raising a force of over 2000 men, mostly from his home estates. This force was called at first Lord MacLeod's Highlanders and later the Highland Light Infantry and Royal Highland Fusiliers. It was in such ways that the Highlands, once a thorn in the side of the House of Hanover, became in a short time one of the major sources of recruitment for the British Army.

Gradually the Cromartie fortunes revived. The parish minister, the same Reverend Colin Mackenzie, had become factor of the estates, and faithfully sent the rents due to the Earl and his family in their times of greatest need. In 1784 the estates were restored.

The Earldom, however, was not revived until 1861, and then it was not a man but a woman who received the title. Ann Hay Mackenzie of Cromartie, Mistress of the Robes, a lady of great charm, was a favourite of Queen Victoria, and, inheriting the estates, was created Countess of Cromartie in her own right. Shortly afterwards she married the Duke of Sutherland, and it was through their second son that the honours were confirmed in their granddaughter Sibel in 1895. Sibel's son, Roderick Grant Francis, the Fourth and present Earl, succeeded in 1962, and has taken great interest in public affairs, local and national. He was the last

COURT OF THE
LORD LYON
SCOTLAND

A PETITION at the INSTANCE of the Right Honourable RODERICK GRANT FRANCIS MACKENZIE OF KINTAIL, Earl of Cromartie, etc., has been PRESENTED in the Court of the Lord Lyon, Scotland (Primo), for recognition of the Petitioner in the name of Mackenzie of Kintail and as Chief of the Clan and Name of Mackenzie; (Secundo) to restore the proper Arms of the Chief of the Mackenzies in the Petitioner's person; and (Tertio) for MATRICULATION of the said Arms in the name of the Petitioner as Chief of the Mackenzies, in which Petition the Lord Lyon King of Arms has pronounced the following INTERLOCUTOR:

Edinburgh, 19th January 1979.
The Lord Lyon King of Arms appoints the Petition to be intimated on the walls and in the Minute Book in common form and to be advertised once in the ' Edinburgh Gazette ' and once in each of ' The Scotsman ' and the ' News of the World ' newspapers and Ordains all parties claiming interest to lodge answers thereto if so advised within forty-two days of such intimation and advertisement.

J. MONTEITH GRANT,
Lyon.

Of all which notice is hereby given.

Sir IAIN MONCREIFFE
OF THAT ILK, Bt.,
Albany Herald of Arms.

Easter Moncreiffe,
Bridge of Earn,
Perthshire.

Convener of the Ross and Cromarty County Council, and the first Convener of the Ross and Cromarty District of the Highland Region. In consequence of his services he had the distinction of being made the first Freeman of the District.

Castle Leod

The wealth and power of the Mackenzies may be gauged by the number of castles and other great houses they have had in Fodderty and neighbouring parishes from the sixteenth century onward. Today the most interesting of these is, of course, Castle Leod. Nigel Tranter describes it as a 'most handsome and commodious house, situated impressively on a green mound in its large and nobly wooded estate.' (Tranter, *The Fortified House in Scotland*)

Because, no doubt, of certain dates inscribed on its walls, it has been assumed by many authorities that it was actually built by Sir Roderick Mackenzie, the famous Tutor of Kintail, in the opening years of the seventeenth century. This, argues the present Earl of Cromartie, is quite inaccurate; the Tutor added the top storey and made other alterations, but there is ample evidence of earlier construction, and it is very unlikely that Sir John, his grandfather, then Chief, would have planted the great chestnut trees in 1550 if there had been no castle there. I have suggested above (page 29) that building on the site was begun by Jarl Olaf the Viking, five hundred years before.

The present castle is of stone, quarried locally, and its walls are seven feet thick. There are gunloops, arrow-slit windows and other windows with iron grilles. According to Stewart Cruden *(The Scottish Castle)* Castle Leod resembles Crathes Castle in being an L-plan tower-house with an unusually large re-entrant stair-tower which is absorbed into the main block, because this stair-tower extends from the re-entrant angle to the gable-end of the principal wing. Cruden also observes that the construction was presumably inspired by the towers of Mar and the Garioch, of which Castle Leod's 'corbelling and other details of considerable richness and variety' are 'strongly reminiscent'.

The trees are, of course, a feature of the policies. The biggest chestnut, 107 feet high, with a girth of 36 feet, is claimed to be the largest of its kind in Great Britain. A second chestnut close by and nearly as large, survived four hundred years to perish in the severe snow-storm of January, 1978, which claimed human life as well. Another remarkable tree is the Wellingtonia, a kind of sequoia grown from a seed imported from America in 1850. In 1965 its

PLANTED c. 1550 BY JOHN MACKENZIE, IXTH CHIEF OF KINTAIL,
1480-1556.
PRIVY COUNCILLOR TO KING JAMES V. AND QUEEN MARY.
GREAT GRANDFATHER TO SIR RODERICK MACKENZIE OF CASTLE LEOD,
COIGACH AND TARBAT, ANCESTOR OF THE EARLS OF CROMARTIE,
1574-1626.
MEASUREMENTS 1966.
GIRTH AT BASE — — — 36 FT.
GIRTH AT 6 FT. 2 INS. — — 28 FT. 2 INS.
LENGTH OF BOLE — — — 18 FT. 6 INS.
SPREAD OF BRANCHES — — 249 FT. (IN 1850)
HEIGHT — — — — — 107 FT.

A SECOND SPANISH CHESTNUT SITUATED 100 YARDS N. W.
OF THIS SPOT PLANTED AT THE SAME TIME MEASURES.
GIRTH AT BASE — — — 24 FT. 6 INS.
GIRTH AT 6 FT. — — — 19 FT. 2 INS.
LENGTH AT BOLE — — — 18 FT.
SPREAD OF BRANCHES — — 246 FT. (IN 1850)
HEIGHT — — — — — 85 FT.

volume was estimated as being 2100 cubic feet, which could make it the largest tree in the United Kingdom.

Other Castles and Houses

'Battlemented Brahan' was demolished after the Second World War.* In its day the castle was a most impressive building with, it is said, a courtyard large enough to drill a thousand men. Built early in the seventeenth century, it was for a long time the home of the Seaforths. From its past have been preserved many relics, including stones with sculptured heraldry and others with the mysterious 'cup marks'. Fortrose Town Hall has become the repository of many interesting Seaforth portraits formerly at Brahan.

Parts of Conon House, originally Logie House, are very old, but most of it was added in 1759. Coul House, Contin, was built in 1821 and is now an hotel. Fairburn Tower, now roofless, was a stronghold of the Mackenzies built about 1600. The door to the

*The present owner of Brahan, no longer a Mackenzie, has converted the stables into a very attractive house.

upper levels is on the first floor. It was on the top floor that the cow gave birth to the calf in 1853, fulfilling the Brahan Seer's prophecy (see page 49).

To the east of where the Kyle Railway climbs up the northern slope of the Strath lay the four davochs, Dochmaluag, Dochcairn, Dochcarty and Dochpollo. A davoch was a piece of land of eight acres. It is a very ancient measure, and these names are recorded as early as 1400. Dochmaluag came into the possession of the Mackenzies from 1476. Dochmaluag Tower, which was garrisoned by Cromwellian troops, stands on Brae Farm. The name of the davoch derives from St Moluag, who is specially associated with the Island of Lismore, but who also had much influence in Easter Ross where he founded Rosemarkie Monastery. A contemporary, perhaps a student of St Columba, he seems to have been the leader of a party which resisted the Roman rule which Columba accepted.

The Brahan Seer

From perusal of the foregoing pages the reader might well come to the conclusion that the Northern Highlands of former times was a scene of constant carnage. Such an impression could well be unbalanced. Every country and every age, not excluding our own, has its record of man's inhumanity to man. But even the ravages of the Vikings on our coasts were no worse than those of the armies of Europe during the Thirty Years War. After all, the most recent Highland atrocities, Glencoe, the post-Culloden butcheries and the Clearances were perpetrated not by, but on the Highland people. Violence makes news while peace and ordinary life go unrecorded. Thus it should not be forgotten that for Lewis and Harris at least, the Middle Ages was a time of comparative peace and agricultural progress, while the fact that Inverness Town Council could make a grant to a noble lord of the time to help him to improve his golf suggests that all was not blood and iron. But the most important factor of all to be taken into consideration is the Highland ideal of character. Nobody would maintain that everbody lived up to it. (Indeed a Highland policeman in Glasgow said, very confidentially, to the present writer 'A bad Highlander is the worst of all!') But one has met in the humblest of circumstances simple folk who, with quiet dignity, exhibited the required characteristics of loyalty, hospitality and humour which are not acquired in a day, but spring from deeply rooted custom and long tradition. Add to this the music, song and story-telling of the Gael and one realises that

Highland life was mostly concerned with far more worthy things than internecine warfare. The section which follows indicates a kind of experience very real to him which the mere recording historian might overlook — a sense of the mystical and unseen.

Part of the value of preserving the Celtic culture, now only found in the western fringe of Europe, is that it is the last remnant of a way of life almost submerged by the modern scientific and secular outlook. What Gaeldom calls 'the Second Sight' is sometimes taken to be a part of this pre-modern culture. The phenomenon is not confined, of course, to the Scottish Highlands. The prophetic writings of the Old Testament and the oracles of the ancient world are examples of the same kind of 'second sight'. The famous Thomas the Rhymer lived in the Scottish Lowlands, and we may recall that when James I was leaving Edinburgh for his ill-fated visit to Perth he was given a fearful warning by a woman that death lay in wait if he proceeded. We need not suppose that this kind of thing belongs to the past. In a village in Central Scotland today resides a woman possessing this faculty. She considers it most distressing, and indeed so afraid and ashamed of it is she that, though stories have leaked out, only her closest associates are aware of her identity. Unlike conventional mediums, such persons try to restrict rather than develop the 'gift', which is said to be hereditary.

In Highland history the best-known person of this type was probably Coinneach Odhar (pronounded Co-in-yeach Ore), Brown Kenneth, the Brahan Seer. A native of Lewis, he came to work on the Brahan Estate in the second half of the seventeenth century. His story in full is found in Elizabeth Sutherland's revision of Alexander Mackenzie's *The Prophecies of the Brahan Seer*.

In recent times the authenticity of the tales and even the identity of the Seer have been in dispute. This is only natural when it is considered that folk history, largely transmitted by word of mouth, tends to cut out complications, so that one central figure often attracts to himself occurrences originally connected with others. This produces internal contradictions and conflicting evidence; yet evidence that conflicts is in itself evidence that something tangible exists in the background. Thus Robert Bain writes, 'that many of his predictions have been proved true by their fulfilment does not admit of question.' Yet Bain also says that Coinneach Odhar was known to have had 'imitators' who might, indeed, have fathered a prophecy on the Seer after the event had taken place.

One of the interesting points about the Highland seers is that they had a penchant for prophesying the doom of their chiefs. Coinneach Odhar was no exception. Of the Seaforth family, with which he had such close ties, he pronounced that the last of the line would be deaf and dumb, his four sons would predecease him, and one of his daughters would kill her sister. The line did become extinct under just such circumstances, the male line in 1815. In 1823 the Hon Caroline Mackenzie was accidentally killed when thrown from her carriage as it was being driven down Brahan Brae by her sister. A monument recording the event stands at the foot of the hill.

A famous prophecy was that of the end of the then powerful Mackenzies of Fairburn Tower. 'They shall disappear almost to a man from the face of the earth. Their castle shall become uninhabited, and a cow shall give birth to a calf in the top chamber of the Tower.' The line did become extinct in 1850, and the next year a cow, following wisps of hay up the stone staircase to where it was stored on the top floor of the now deserted building, refused to descend and eventually produced a calf. The *Inverness Courier* of the time records how the event so impressed the townspeople that special excursions were organised to observe the curious phenomenon.

About the end of the Seer himself the usual story is as follows: Having been summoned from Strathpeffer to Brahan by Lady Seaforth to entertain her guests, he reluctantly disclosed that her consort was at that moment on his knees making love to a young lady in Paris. Accordingly, the Seer was apprehended and burnt in a barrel of tar at Chanonry Point near Fortrose. The accuracy of this version is, however, strongly contested and it seems likely that the Seer was confused with a person of the same name a century earlier in time, connected with the House of Munros of Foulis. In the records of the latter dated 1577/8 there appears a Note of Commission appointing (various persons) 'judiciaries to apprehend, imprison and try Kenneth Owir, leader in the art of magic (and others) as shall be named by the ministers within the bounds'. Elizabeth Sutherland argues that it was this earlier Coinneach Odhar (who would be a very serious warlock in a superstitious age) who met his end at Chanonry, and she believes that a stone discovered in a garden near the present golf-course marks the spot of execution. Bain does not seem to know about this earlier Kenneth, but sensing, perhaps, that some of the stories about the Brahan Seer were not in character, writes that 'he was a good, even a pious man, and as innocent of sorcery as of coining.' (*loc cit*). Furthermore, Hugh Miller, born in Cromarty in 1802 (perhaps within a century of the Seer's death), tells us that he ended his days wandering about the countryside, living into extreme old age.

Some of the Brahan Seer's prophecies were of a general nature, though of course they would not have gained authority unless this mere peasant had established a reputation by more immediate impact.

'One day fire and water will run through the streets of Inverness' (gas, electricity and piped water supply).

'Long lines of carriages without horses will run between Inverness and Dingwall and Skye' (the railways).

'One day, uninviting as it is now, the time will come when this well shall be under lock and key, and crowds will throng to obtain a draught of its waters.' (Strathpeffer as a Spa).

Perhaps the present writer may conclude this section with a personal note. One of the Seer's prophecies which has persisted down the years is that when the Eagle Stone falls the third time ships will come sailing up the valley and be moored to it. In its present position, high up the hillside such an event is so impossible that one wondered how the legend refused to die. When recently, however, the writer learned that the stone had previously stood beside the Tympan Mill at the foot of the garden of Ardival House where he himself had spent most of his boyhood the situation was altered, for the waters which turned the mill-wheel are of course in the valley. He thought about the new position and suddenly realised it was on the edge of the railway station policies and within a few yards of where the trains used to stop. Might the seer's psychic sense of a large vehicle approaching and disgorging passengers not have been caused, not by a ship, but a railway engine and carriages? In any case the local people were so impressed by the Seer's extra sense that they took the trouble of moving the stone to a more secure place up the hill where it now stands.*

---

* Lord Cromartie tells us that in his family there is a legend that after a skirmish in which the Mackenzies defeated the Munros the former took the Eagle Stone from wherever it had previously been and chivalrously marked with it the massed graves of their slain opponents whose clan crest happened to be the eagle. If so the present stone must be in its third site at least. The Ardival gully could mark the site of the battle and some digging might produce positive evidence of what at present must remain conjectural.

Whatever we may think of such a notion, the continuing strength of belief in the veracity of Coinneach Odhar's predictions is testified to by the front page of the *People's Journal* for September 23, 1978.

The report relates how the Highland Regional Council's Planning Committee, bedevilled by traffic congestion, had been considering the advisability of building another bridge across the River Ness at Inverness. The river is already spanned by six bridges. A ratepayer with a long memory telephoned one of the members of the committee to ask whether he knew that the Brahan Seer had prophesied destruction for the town by fire and water and the fall of black rain in the event of the construction of a seventh bridge across the Ness. The good councillors were preparing to laugh it off when someone pointed out that 'black rain' could mean radioactive fall-out from a nuclear disaster at Dounreay. Sobered, the committee ordered the costing of the alternative of tunnelling under the river![*]

---

[*] Moreover, Mrs Winnie Ewing, SNP Euro-candidate for the Highlands and Islands, is reported in the press recently as blaming the recent foul weather on the Prime Minister, since the Brahan Seer foretold that when two women ruled the kingdom summer would turn into winter!

3. After the 'Forty-five

The Life of the People

After the Jacobite Rebellion had been crushed there was a period of much hardship throughout the Highlands. The clan system was not modern democracy, but it was a far more closely knit and friendly community life than feudalism provided. The chief did regard himself as the father of the clan and could be relied on to be concerned with the need of his humblest follower. This position was something like that of Abraham and other patriarchs in the Old Testament. The clan chief was father of a great family even if some of its members were not blood relations. The loyalty of clansmen to their chief, correspondingly, was quite remarkable. There was not the sense of personal ownership which marks modern acquisitive society. All had access to moor and stream in seeking the necessities of life. To this day many Highlanders cannot be persuaded that poaching is anything but an honourable profession. That the Laird should have his castle and immediate possessions was not disputed but who, they would argue, gave him exclusive right to game or salmon, which, like the air we breathe surely belongs to all — though, they would readily agree, there are certain forms of organised poaching which are entirely abhorrent. The people therefore tended to be pastoral rather than agricultural.

After the 'Forty-five the government introduced laws to destroy the old loyalties. Even Highland dress was banned. When therefore more peaceable times returned and the castle was occupied again by the rightful owner, the relationship that had once been between chief and clansman was now that of proprietor and tenant. At the end of the eighteenth century it was remarked that there were eight proprietors in the Strath, not one of whom had ever resided in it. This was not always the fault of the absentee since he might be under sentence of banishment or other disability, but it helps one to understand the vacuum which now existed in the centuries-old outlook of the people.

The crofter had now to depend on his small allotment for a living and though he worked hard this was insufficient. We are told that in May and June great numbers of country folk left home to work elsewhere and when they returned in November they would only have from 10s to 42s as the fruit of their labour. At home the wages of men were seldom more than 6d a day though we should remember that beef and mutton cost 3d a pound, a pound of pork 2½d and fowls 4d each. Young men joined the army in great numbers and whole families emigrated to become the ancestors of many now prosperous citizens of Canada, New Zealand and elsewhere.

Under the new order many lairds did not themselves find things very easy economically since their estates were large and often unproductive. But at this point there came a rise in the price of wool and many landowners, now much more in touch with the outside world, saw the opportunity to improve their condition. So began the story of the Clearances. That at least the lower end of the Strath did not escape unscathed from the bitterness of the era is testified in John Prebble's book *The Highland Clearances*.

> One man, a respectable miller, whose father and grandfather had rented a mill in Fodderty parish, having taken the part of a poor woman ejected from her holding and driven from the landlord's door with a stick, walked ten miles yesterday to tell us of his own case. In the midst of a winter's night, with deep snow on the ground, he and his aged mother were suddenly turned out of his house, and his mother is now bedridden in consequence.

But the Strath as a whole came through better than many areas. For at least part of the time the parish minister, the Rev Colin Mackenzie, was acting as factor for the forfeited Cromartie estates and both he and his sons did fine work in bringing more prosperity to the district. The Earl's son, Lord MacLeod, was an officer very anxious to prove his loyalty to the government and he got a very favourable response from the young men of the Fodderty parish when he advertised for recruits for the British Army engaged in the American War of Independence. When they returned home many of them were settled in the Heights of Achterneed. Some years later when there was much suffering caused by the evictions from Strathconon the Cromartie Estate authorities who had been intending to create two new large farms decided instead to break up the areas and divide them among these homeless people.

54

Old Mill, Milnum, Stradbroke, William Hutchins.

The crofting people right up to recent days worked long and hard. An author at the beginning of the last century writes that 'Sloth seems to be the greatest enemy to the morality of the people here', but the present writer can only leave it on record that when still a boy and visiting some of the crofts he noted the floors of beaten earth, the lack of common amenities and good people often bent with toil.

In earlier times conditions would have been even more primitive. The usual cottage was called a 'long-house' and provided accommodation for man and beast. The two sections would be partitioned off. The peat fire, never in a lifetime allowed to go out, would be in the centre of the humans' floor-space. Peat smoke does not linger at lower levels and in this case escaped through a hole in the roof. Originally there was seldom a table, meals being taken round the fire, often with communal dishes. There was little pottery, bowls and other containers usually being made of wood. Above the fire there hung the cooking pot, suspended by a strong iron chain, the weight of which could indicate the wealth of the family.

Housing conditions in the country districts of the Strath were considerably in advance of those further west. Well-built, substantial manses and farmhouses made people familiar with higher standards of domestic living. Fireplaces were inserted in cottage gables and livestock quarters separated from those of humans, vacated space becoming a separate room. From early times, too, there had always been an area used as a workshop and, since most people were craftsmen of one kind or another, there was a wide range of skills at their disposal. Once upon a not too distant time they spun their own thread, dyed their own wool, wove their own cloth and tailored their own garments — primitive, no doubt, but independent.

Colin MacDonald, whose widow died as recently as 1978, describes in his *Echoes of the Glen* the life of the people on the Heights of Achterneed as he knew it in his boyhood. Before 1870, he tells us, in the fifty crofts of the district there was no way of beating out the grain but by the flail, nor any means of separating grain from chaff but by winnowing (that is, by placing the pile between two open doors and hoping for an obliging wind!). The first hand-mill did not appear till 1872.

Chaff was not thrown away but was put into large sacks which for the next year served as welcome mattresses for the board-bottomed beds.

Oatmeal was the staple diet among the great bulk of country people, and wages were often paid in meal and milk. Meal of course made porridge. This was not the tame watery concoction common in more refined places in the south. Into boiling water a steady stream of meal was stirred for about ten minutes. Salt was added and another ten minutes allowed for simmering. It was then served immediately, each spoonful of porridge being dipped by the eater into a bowl of milk. While lumps were not favoured, the average Highlander liked his porridge thick.

Products of oats included other items such as bannocks or oatcakes, gruel, sowens* and stapag˙. Brose was a dish to which the writer was addicted as a boy. Nothing, except a boiled egg, could be simpler in preparation: some meal in a bowl with a pinch of salt, boiling water stirred in to achieve the consistency of stiff dough, a cover briefly placed over for a not very apparent reason, milk poured on — and there's your breakfast!

Oatmeal was basic to a degree we can scarcely comprehend nowadays. As late as the middle of the last century, in a small town like Dingwall there were several shops which sold nothing else. However, a barrel of salted herring was the great standby in many crofting homes; without it, the day's main meals were chiefly porridge and potatoes; with it, as Colin MacDonald observes, they were chiefly porridge, potatoes and herring!**

Rabbits seem to have been a late importation, not appearing in Gairloch until 1850. Pigs were a good investment with a speedy turnover and, Norman Macrae tells us, come into the picture from the seventeenth century. So popular were they that even in the town of Dingwall nearly every house had its sty. Apparently, however, certain elements in the population had religious scruples similar to those of the Jews: a century ago there were 2,692 pigs in Easter Ross, but in the Island of Lewis there were only two! Little beef was available, but when an animal was killed, all the carcass, flesh, bones, blood, skin, entrails and the rest were used for one purpose or another.

As for other food, milk was essential, and eggs in universal use.

*A dish made by steeping and fermenting the husks, 'seeds' or siftings of oats in water, and then boiling *(Chambers Scots Dictionary)*.

†A mixture of oat-meal and cold water, 'drammock' *(Chambers Scots Dictionary)*.

**It was not only the Scottish Highlander who was so dependent on oats. In one of the largest and most popular restaurants in Belfast as late as the 1950's porridge was on the menu not only for breakfast but also for high tea.

Until recent times gardens were not cultivated perhaps to the fullest extent possible, but river and moor from time to time produced their delicacies. Berries and nuts were plentiful in season. Children did not hesitate to help themselves when passing a turnip field, declaring, very rightly, that turnips were more tasty uncooked.

Customs and Standards

Community spirit was good, as we have already said in connection with even earlier times. In the period under discussion peat cutting, for example, was still a community undertaking and distribution shared by all. The old and needy were generously supplied. Indeed, their requirements would be the first to be taken into consideration. No geriatric problem in the modern sense existed since a spirit of interdependence permeated all. The old tradition of the open house was kept up, and neighbours came and went freely whether to give unstinted help to the failing and the infirm or to enliven a winter's evening with a ceilidh. No intrusive cathode ray tube for them! The living traditions of the North in story and song, interpreted by their own voices, were sufficient entertainment for the Highlanders of the Strath and elsewhere. With a little imagination we can see them, their faces sharply etched in the flickering firelight against the shadows, their hands and feet beating time to some ancient rhythm under the bening presidency of the goodman of the house, his home-made chair raised a little above the rest; apart from this, and the fact that the goodwife would also have her special place of honour, there was little formality in seating arrangements and all arrivals were given the same welcome.

In earlier times the clarsach, or Highland harp, provided the main musical accompaniment. Later the fiddle became very popular. Dancing, save in the castle, would be out of doors until the coming of the public hall.

In the more recent period of Strathpeffer's history, morals had improved considerably. At the time of the *Second Statistical Account* (1838), the Rev John Noble of Fodderty Parish tells us that in the preceding three years only six illegitimate births had occurred; considering the mobility of labour, this was less than might have been expected. During his time family worship in the manner described in Burns' 'Cotter's Saturday Night' was usual. Visitors might come and go but this was routine, accepted by all, with the singing of a metrical psalm, reading of scripture and prayer led by the head of the house.

Mr Noble does complain, however, that the parishioners were much addicted to the use of spirits and would go to every length to procure them. Indolent persons often used dishonest means for supplying their lack. The Rev Mr Noble relates how a sheep went missing and suspicion fell immediately on a local man with a bad reputation in such matters. The culprit guessed that justice was on his tracks and, having sent his wife and small child out of the way, killed the sheep, placed it in the cradle and covered it with a blanket. When the investigators arrived, they found their quarry sitting rocking the cradle and complaining loudly that his wife had left him with so menial a task. Being then sharply interrogated about the missing animal, he protested indignantly, '*Is cho luath churrain sgian anns na tha sa chreal ghaoidin a chaora.*' ('Me steal a sheep! I would as soon stick a knife into what is in this cradle!') The visitors searched the premises in vain and took their departure, sadder but no wiser men. It is significant that this story was told as a joke.

Although puritanism took over so completely in one way, in the Highlands a strong sense of the supernatural remained from the ancient past. If the observance of Christmas is forbidden on the grounds that the date of Christ's birth is unknown, it is inevitable that the purely secular or even pre-Christian observance of New Year has a greater chance of survival. The season of All Saints was not recognised by the Church but Hallowe'en was vigorously, even violently, observed, and ghostly figures arrayed in strange disguise passed from house to house. In May, Beltane fires, lit by combustion produced by the friction of two pieces of wood, celebrated the coming of summer. On the first day of the month maidens in search of beauty rose betimes to wash their faces in the dew.

The great day was in January — not the first, but the twelfth (the old New Year). The great feature of this in the Strath was an annual shinty match played by twenty or more men a side. The contestants would fashion their own camans, or shinty-sticks, from suitably shaped tree branches. The game is claimed to be one of the oldest in existence with a continuous history. It resembles hockey in some ways but came to Scotland with the Gaels from Ireland where it is still popular and called 'hurling'. Both countries have codified the laws of the respective games and, with necessary adjustments, play an annual international match.

Till very recent times there was a deep dread of the 'taisg' or wraith which was ever on the search for young children to steal or exchange. Some years ago a lady visitor to the Spa, plainly dressed but actually of considerable means, was accosted while out walking by a couple of women who handed over a small parcel with the remark 'Would you mind taking this? We've just had a baptism.' Much mystified the recipient took the package back to her hotel to find that it contained a few slices of bread and some pieces of cake. It was explained to her by others present that this was an old custom observed after the party following an infant's baptism and was supposed to preserve the child from evil. No doubt originally it had been an offering to the 'taisg'. Whether the child in the case benefited we do not know; certainly the lady recipient did not because she repeated several times, 'So that's what people think of me! That's what people think of me!'*

In the eighteenth and nineteenth centuries religion played an important part in moulding the character and outlook of the people. The tolerance and mysticism of earlier times blended well enough with the discipline of Calvinism, and still gives strength to the spiritual conception of what life is about. But there have been times when preachers, possibly with the best of intentions, have not hesitated to exploit the sensitivity of their listeners especially with regard to eternal punishment. One itinerant who could attract crowds had as his three points: (1) The intolerable agony of even one moment of Hell; (2) That even after a century of suffering one was no nearer the end than at the beginning; (3) That however good one might try to be, unless one were of the 'elect', nothing could save one from perdition. Colin MacDonald in *Echoes of the Glen* describes how, as a small boy at bedtime, he clung to his mother, both of them in tears, so filled were they with terror.

Round about 1800 all the residents in the parish belonged to Fodderty Parish Church except for two who were Episcopalian. It is interesting to note that about the same time everybody in the parish spoke Gaelic fluently, except two. We are not told if they were the Episcopalians! By the end of the century only the elderly and middle-aged could usually be presumed to be so efficient in the language of old Gaul. Today, save for incomers, there is nobody. And, sadly, with the language has largely gone the way of life.

To give the impression that English was a completely alien

*This is not just a 'Highland' tradition; it is possibly more widespread in the industrial lowlands of the South.

tongue would not be accurate. Inverness people always maintain that their ancestors learnt their English from Cromwell's soldiers. These and later English troops garrisoned fortresses further north including several in our own parish. But even before that Inverness was a busy seaport with English ships calling in frequently, and there were certainly English settlers in the district in early times. These people made their contribution to the community and left their influence to this day. There are still people in the Strath who talk of 'traycle', 'bate' and 'mate' (food) etc. instead of treacle, beat and meat. Furthermore, when children say they are 'starving' they are far more likely to be very cold than very hungry. This is not the misuse of a noble tongue but the English of John Milton and William Shakespeare.

Health

The health of the community was by many standards quite robust, especially if we think of other times and places such as city slums. This is not surprising, if we consider how much the people led active lives, ate natural food and were out in the open air. Norman Macrae in his *Romance of a Royal Burgh* quotes an ancient Gaelic proverb 'Is righ gach slan' ('Every healthy man is a king') and indeed good health was taken by many as the norm. The present writer in high school days lodged in the home of a blacksmith of this stock. At least eighty years of age, he was able to do a full day's work at the forge, and used to be proud of the fact that he still retained in perfect condition all thirty-two teeth in his head.

When illness did strike, common sense, folk surgery and folk medicine occupied the place later taken by modern scientific medicine. Macrae lists the following herbs as being useful: 'mint for flatulence, burnt cakes for indigestion, foxglove for a weak heart, broom-tops and juniper berries for the kidneys, dandelion roots for a purge . . .', all acceptable, we understand, to orthodox medical practice. The bone-setter, now called an osteopath, who had learned his skill largely by experience, often was a person of astonishing accomplishments who could, by his art, relieve conditions serious even by today's medical standards.

Some forms of treatment sprang from common sense; others were beneficial for reasons other than those supposed. A hot meal poultice applied to the soles of the feet helped indirectly by making the patient in a feverish condition stay in bed. On the other hand an elderly couple of the author's acquaintance, on the onset of a cold or worse, sought, lightly dressed, the windiest hillside available!

Their survival proves something, though what the orthodox book would say about it we do not know. When we remember that near-magic methods were also in use we have to recall that in healing there are many psychological and perhaps spiritual factors.

Yet we should be very grateful for modern medicine. If many healthy people were to be seen, one should not forget these were often survivors of large families. Nowadays, if we subtract the devastations of tobacco, alcoholism and motor transport, most people die simply because age has worn out their vital organs. Not so of old. Death struck all ages and classes in the Strath. Before the days of insulin, I remember seeing a diabetic schoolboy so thin that he seemed but a walking skeleton. Tuberculosis in our healthy community seemed not to have many victims but infectious disease struck with awful suddenness and effect. Our much loved Rory the Postman lost two lovely children, as did a local solicitor. The manse lost one child and kept a second stricken by deafness. One day things were normal but, within a week, a home was filled with tragedy. It is therefore interesting to read a comment from the beginning of the nineteenth century:

> There are no distempers peculiar to the parish except such as are common to the neighbouring places. The smallpox often rages here, and frequently proves mortal, as innoculation has never been attempted except by a very few families, who recently introduced it with success. The prejudice of the people is, however very strong against.

People can be very slow to learn.

Not everybody's teeth were perfect. Toothache abounded until the sufferer, far from a dentist's care, had summoned up enough courage to have the molar extracted — of course without anaesthetic. Furthermore in those times it was accepted that with age came serious impairment of eyesight and possibly hearing. Today conditions that once caused complete blindness can very satisfactorily be overcome and, of course, deaf-aids can bring the dull of hearing back into the stream of life even when physical betterment is as yet beyond medical knowledge. Today many grannies, lightly clad, may disport themselves on the golf-course, but in previous times people over sixty, whether fit or not, were expected to behave as those in the final stage of life. As far as the old women were concerned, at least, they were so weighed down with garments that flightiness was out of the question. When poor folk could not afford dentures their sunken countenances advertised to the whole world the hopelessness of their condition. Almost to our own time, Shakespeare's picture of age was only too accurate: 'Sans teeth, sans eyes, sans taste, sans everything.' The good old days had their sombre side.

Ecclesiastical

The ecclesiastical history of the parish is quite interesting. Fodderty churchyard, though on the main road half-way between Dingwall and Strathpeffer, seems a rather isolated place. From earliest time it has marked a sacred spot. Many parish churches, of course, were built on sites previously hallowed by pre-Christian religions and this may well have been the case with Fodderty. But round about the year 1000 it had a specially strategic position at the top end of the Brae Fiord, or Cromarty Firth, which in former times extended much further inland than now. After the church had gone, the graveyard still remained, and for at least one thousand years it has been the last resting place not only for the folk of its own parish but also for many from Dingwall itself. Its situation would make it a prime setting for the supernatural, and indeed there is the legend of a frenzied wraith looking in vain for her lost lover. Woe betide the traveller arriving on the scene after dark!*

After covenanting times it was not for a long time customary to have religious services at burials. As a reaction against what they considered superstitious rites, the puritanical elements in Presbyterianism held that services should be in the home only and for the comfort of the living. The dead were now in God's hands, and beyond the power of the Church to aid any more. Burials thus had no religious content and became mere secular engagements. Hospitality was not, however, stinted and, long distances having sometimes to be travelled, there were often occasions of over-indulgence in drink. There is a story of such a group proceeding from the Garve to Ullapool and finding at the end of the journey that their Burden, the disposal of which had been the purpose of their journey had been left behind at some intermediate point! Of course there have been great changes in more recent times. But it is still remembered that it was a good long trek, two and a half miles,

---

*A collection of beliefs of this sort belonging to Easter Ross (none actually referring to Fodderty) is to be found in Hugh Miller's *Scenes and Legends of the North of Scotland* (1858), chapter XXV.

perhaps in inclement weather, from Strathpeffer to Fodderty. The hearse and one or two horse-drawn carriages went first, followed on foot by most of the male relatives and acquaintances of the deceased. In the case of a prominent citizen's death this could mean a whole morning or afternoon off work for many people. Why not, indeed? It showed that all individuals did count and that one's passing was significant for the whole community.

A few years ago the present writer happened to be in the vicinity of Fodderty churchyard when the funeral was to take place of a friend of former days. The latter had run a successful business which had been in the family for several generations, and he was well known in a wide area. His name was Mackenzie and his brother's name was on the memorial gates' roll of honour. There is now a large parking area beside the churchyard and not only was this completely occupied, but the line of other parked cars stretched along the road almost out of sight. In a city the corresponding final tribute often tends to be somewhat casual, but in the Strath, I felt, the one who had gone still had a living, loving connection among friends. He was born of their stock, lived and served among them and at the end was not separated from them.

> Home is the sailor, home from the sea,
> And the hunter home from the hill.

The Churches

The present parish of Fodderty was originally three, Fodderty and Kinnettas churches being in or beside where the churchyards now are and Tollie on the other side of Knockfarrel. When one considers the position of surrounding parish churches, Dingwall, Conon (probably), Urray and Contin it is realised that few people would have much more than a mile to go to the church. With the Reformation changes, higher academic standards were required of the clergy, whose numbers were consequently reduced. So the three local churches were united in about 1600 under Fodderty. Since then all three church buildings have disappeared, Tollie under the waters of Loch Ussie when it was enlarged to become Dingwall's water supply, and the others by demolition. Fodderty's church was dedicated to St Mary though this may originally have been St Maelrubha, the patron saint of Loch Maree. But Fodderty was not very central and a new building was erected a mile further up the Strath.

The replacement church was restored and adapted at the beginning of the last century. It was originally designed to hold four hundred but to accommodate parishioners coming down over Knockfarrel it was enlarged to hold two hundred more. We are told that the church was full at its services and if we remember that these offered a choice between English and Gaelic it is obvious that the church was central to community life. The original manse at Fodderty is now a guest-house; the new one, now a private house, was built in 1794 opposite the hamlet of Blairninich.

By the end of the nineteenth century the large number of summer visitors at the Spa necessitated the holding of services there and it became obvious that a church must be erected where most of the people were. So was built the present Parish Church which is, internally at least, one of the finest post-Reformation Presbyterian churches in the north. It has several features of architectural note including the fact that all the windows are of different design. The absence of a central aisle, it is said, was a condition imposed at the time of building. The previous building still stands, a very handsome edifice next to Fodderty School. It has been converted into a guest-house and contains in its grounds the two famous cup-marked standing stones.

In the early years of last century there was only one church in the Strath. A century later there were no less than four, all of different denominations. The Disruption of 1843 was caused by too much government control of the Parish Church. The Clearances had embittered many Highlanders against their landlords and since these, who paid the tiends towards the ministers' stipends, also claimed the right to appoint clergy to vacant charges, one third of the ministers left the Establishment and with their followers set up the Free Church of Scotland. In the Highlands the breakaway was much greater than in the South, often including ninety percent of the church members. When the latter, however, wished to build a church for themselves they did not always find the proprietors willing to provide them with a site.

In the case of Strontian in Argyll this was altogether refused and so, not to be outdone, the congregation had a boat to hold six hundred people built on the Clyde at the cost of £1400. One could always calculate how many were in the church by how low the boat was in the water! This situation did not arise with regard to Fodderty, for they managed to secure a piece of ground at Jamestown at the junction with the adjacent parishes of Contin and Urray and the three congregations united to build a church on the spot.

As a matter of fact it was a London businessman and local

Elrick House, Stratpeffer Youth Hostel.

Alla-Haldane.

proprietor, Mr Hugh Matheson of Little Scatwell, who forwarded the Free Church cause in the Spa itself. He had purchased Elsick House, home of Dr Morrison who had so much to do with the opening of the first pump room and began there a Sunday school. He then obtained from the Countess of Cromartie (later the Duchess of Sutherland) ground opposite the present hairdresser's establishment on which to erect a hall. Daily services were held there during the season attended by two to three hundred people. In due course (1887) the present church dominating the square was erected, a handsome structure of Scandinavian dignity and severity very appropriate to our northern latitude. Timorous people were full of doubts. Was its tall steeple secure? From time to time the Strath is subject to earth tremors, so, what if . . .? And should the bell be rung on Sundays? It is a good bell and can be distinctly heard at Keppoch two miles away. Indeed, as late as between the two world wars it was rung four times every Sunday: at 9 in the morning the Waking Bell sounded; at 11 am and 6 pm it rang for the English services; and at 12.20 pm it rang for the Gaelic Service, when the group of elderly people sitting under the beech tree in the square eased themselves off a bench and proceeded uphill.

In 1900 the Free Church of Scotland united with the United Presbyterian Church to make the United Free Church. But the United Presbyterian Church scarcely existed in the Highlands and was somewhat suspect to the Free Church; the ironic result was that in Strathpeffer as in many other northern parishes the 'Union' of 1900 meant another division! The Strathpeffer section entering the Union had then to build themselves a suite of buildings of their own which was quite comparable with their neighbours. When this denomination united with the Parish Church in 1929 the two sets of buildings were not necessary. The UF manse was retained as that of the united charge, but the spire and nave of that church were demolished, and the remainder with the halls were converted into a very attractive private hotel.

The Episcopal Church is often referred to as the English Church. This designation is not quite accurate. As late as 1700 we know that the majority of Dingwall people favoured the episcopal form of church government and, though the misfortunes following the Jacobite Rebellion eventually led to the majority accepting the rule of the presbytery, there has always been an indigenous Episcopalian strain from which the county families have seldom wavered. Summer

67

visitors from England guaranteed reasonably good attendances at least for half the year, and in 1892 the present beautiful St Anne's Church was opened as a memorial to the late Duchess of Sutherland, first Countess of Cromartie in her own right. The church is a dependent mission worked by the rector of St James's, Dingwall. It has seating for three hundred. There is a fine pipe organ, an altar of sculptured marble and a carved stone pulpit. Twenty-one very fine stained glass windows are among the many gifts with which the church is endowed. There is a peal of eight small bells.

Nowadays Strathpeffer is well-known in the church world as the home of the Northern Convention which annually attracts large numbers of people from all parts of the country.

The Clerics

Ecclesiastically, probably the best known of the clerics associated with the Strath was Rev John MacKillican who was inducted to Fodderty in 1656 but deprived in 1662. This was the age of the Covenanters and the issues debated so hotly seem small to us today; the forms of worship were precisely the same in both orders, and nearer that of the present day Free Presbyterian Church than modern Church of Scotland and Episcopalian services. On the surface the sole point of difference was the acceptability or otherwise of bishops in church government. Probably, however, there were underlying emotions at work, with the Covenanters being the more fervid and pastorally committed. In any case MacKillican was one of the many in Scotland who did not shun a martyr's role. He was twice imprisoned on the Bass Rock and died shortly afterwards.

MacKillican was succeeded at Fodderty by no fewer than five Mackenzies. Two of these are specially worthy of note for the contribution they made to the development of Strathpeffer in the ninety-one years between the induction of Colin in 1735 to the death of his son and successor, Donald, in 1826. They themselves belonged to county stock: Colin in due course inherited Dingwall Castle, the ruins of which he largely demolished, and in 1765 he purchased the Aberdeenshire estate of Glack. It was while he was acting as factor for the Cromartie estates that he was instrumental in having steps taken to protect the 'Strong Well'. He dissuaded his relative the Earl of Seaforth from joining the '45 Rising, and while the Earl of Cromartie was banished from Scotland for the rest of his life, Colin Mackenzie saw to the collection of his rents which he duly forwarded to the gallant Countess who had saved her husband so heroically from a terrible end.

Having had a long and extremely active life, the reverend gentleman did not go out with a whimper either, for at the age of ninety-five he preached at the opening of Ferintosh Church.

Colin had two sons of interest to our story, Donald becoming first his father's assistant, then his successor. The brother, Forbes, had a daughter, who married Dr John Kennedy, Dingwall's most famous minister (a monument to his memory may be seen in the church grounds, opposite the railway station), and another who, as we relate elsewhere, founded for Nicolson Memorial Hospital, Strathpeffer. Donald and Forbes were interested in developing the marshy ground in the valley below Achterneed — a relic of the days when the sea came up to this point. The brothers got busy using the new techniques then being employed all over Scotland. Twenty years of hard work ensued, draining, ploughing and re-ploughing, and clearing the ground of stones. Finally lime was necessary, so advantage was taken of the demolition of Dingwall Castle to transfer no fewer than seven hundred cartloads of mortar from the rubble. The transformation of the valley was astonishing. Visitors in the 1830's wrote 'It was, till within a few years, a low marshy valley, occupied by stagnant waters, large reeds, and a few stunted alders. Now it yields the most luxuriant crops of grain, and is one of the richest and best peopled districts in the country.' Such was the achievement of Donald and Forbes Mackenzie. Forbes was accredited with being the first to grow wheat north of the Moray Firth and the first to introduce Clydesdale horses and shorthorn cattle to the Highlands. He was also concerned with the importing of cheviot sheep. Donald, it is recorded, had rather a tragic end. Having climbed steps to reach a book in his library, he slipped and came down so heavily that he died a few days later.

On the Free Church side a figure of some note was Rev W S McDougall, an Irishman by birth and a man greatly respected for his piety. He was responsible in having Mr Moody, the famous American evangelist, visit the Spa on more than one occasion. An open-air gathering, it is said was attended 'by a vast crowd', who were deeply influenced.

Mr McDougall had an astonishing experience one rainy day about which the reader may care to hear. He, his two daughters and the church elder were proceeding to the presbytery at Dingwall by pony and phaeton (an open four-wheeled carriage). As they reached the top of the Elsick Hill — the manse was at Jamestown — the minister got down to adjust the pony's harness. The animal, however, was startled, and leapt ahead, knocking him down so that the wheels passed over him, breaking his leg. The elder was thrown out, injuring his shoulder, while one of the sisters succeeded in jumping clear without harm. The other young lady kept her seat and was borne onwards as the pony, unchecked, careered downhill the full five miles to Dingwall, passing, says our informant, all the carts and carriages in the way. When he came to the middle of the High Street a crowd tried to stop him, but he rushed down a narrow lane where he had to halt. Annie came out quite safe, no injury to herself or the conveyance. Meantime, up in Strathpeffer the family were in suspense wondering what might have happened to their missing daughter. Eventually a telegram arrived, 'Miss McDougall is safe', which reminds us that in 1882 there were no telephones!

4.   The Spa
The Story of its Development

The great importance of wells to early communities is shown in the supernatural beliefs and practices which usually grow up around the basic function of assuaging thirst in such communities. The Strath has had more than its share of springs and wells fitting into most categories. Just across from Fodderty churchyard at the foot of Knockfarrel is the Well of St John the Baptist, the waters of which are specially pure and refreshing. Of old it was reputed to have healing properties and visitors flocking there seeking cures for themselves or their friends were expected to leave a gift, often a fragment of clothing. If the reader wishes a startling contemporary example he has only to drive through the Black Isle when he will find on the southern side of the main road just above Munlochy the most astonishing array of thousands of pieces of cloth hanging around a spring, though most of the contributions are now made by tourists from distant places. A similar phenomenon may be seen at Culloden near the Battlefield whither, on the first Sunday in May, many citizens of Inverness travel out to the 'Clootie Well' to make their offering of a rag and some money — nowadays jocularly, though their ancestors did so seriously. Robert Burns reminds us that 'Clootie' was one of the old Scottish names for the Devil; originally, then, this rite may have been of much deeper significance than realised by the holiday-maker today.

The Strath of course has its own special wells. These are of two distinct kinds, sulphur and chalybeate (iron), and are to be found in various parts of the valley but mainly concentrated in the area of what is now called The Square. The sulphur wells are of different degrees of strength and in the high days of the Spa were numbered one to four.

People were frequenting the wells in considerable numbers at the end of the seventeenth century but the first practical step to respond

71

The Square
Strathpeffer
Allan Haldane

to the popular need was not undertaken until the local minister had the vital area fenced off to prevent pollution by cattle. In 1777 the Rev Colin Mackenzie who was not only minister of the parish but, as we have seen, factor of the Cromartie estates, wrote to the Commissioners concerned as follows:

The Memorial and Representation of Colin Mackenzie, Factor upon the Annexed Estate of Cromartie, humbly sheweth:

That some years ago a fine Mineral Well was discovered on the lands of Ardival, in the Barony of Strathpeffer, and some of the country people from curiosity and partly on account of some disorders they laboured under, continued to drink this water and found it totally removed the complaints. This drew the attention of several of the better sort of people . . . and Dr Alexander Mackenzie of New Tarbat communicated with Dr Donald Munro at London who wrote a treatise which stands recorded among the Transactions of the Royal Society . . .

It is certain beyond doubt that this water creates an appetite and digestion, and it is a remarkable cure for scorbutic or other disorders in the blood, swellings, ulcers, etc. The memorialist knows of two instances — one of William Smith, Master of the Grammar School of Fortrose, and the other of Angus Sutherland, tacksman, of Kincardine — who were both so lame and feeble that they were obliged to be carried to the Well on feather beds in carts; but by the use of the water for some weeks they so recovered as to be able to walk upon their own legs for miles. The Well, consequently, has been pretty much frequented by different ranks of people from Sutherland to Aberdeen.

But the want of accommodation near the Well for the better people discourages many. The memorialist therefore, humbly submits to the Honourable Board whether it would not be proper for the ladies and gentlemen resorting to the Well, to build a good House, Kitchen and Stable — either upon the Farm of Kinnettas, or upon the Lands of Ardguie, both of them dry, wholesome well-aired places, . . . abounding with agreeable and romantic walks, and having very fine goat pasture within half a mile of them.

This house would (also) be of great use to the whole Barony of Strathpeffer. It would be the means of affording them a ready market for their wares, butter, cheese, eggs, milk, kid, lamb, mutton and poultry; and would . . . enable them to pay their rents more punctually than usual, nor is it impossible that in time this place might become a thriving village.

The minister of the parish erected a kind of building about this Well to preserve it from being abused from cattle etc, which by no means answers the end. By laying out £5 or £6 a proper building might be erected.

I wish to God half-a-dozen of the Honourable Board (for pleasure only) tried it for three weeks — they would get an appetite, a pack of good hounds, and plenty of game, goat, whey etc. There would be little occasion for soliciting a support to the enclosed Memorial Representation.

The Commissioners were indeed very impressed with the memorial and made further enquiries with encouraging results. But nothing practical ensued until twenty years had passed: Dr Morrison of Elsick, Aberdeenshire, who himself had long been troubled with arthritis and had visited most of the English spas in vain search of help, tried Strathpeffer, receiving immediate alleviation, and decided to take up residence at the head of the Strath. He then exerted all his energies and public spirit towards making the benefits of the Spa more widely available to the wider world.

In 1819 a wooden pump room, 40 feet long, was built and a regular service established. Visitors on arrival put down their name and paid 2s per week for attendance. The poor were not charged. The Pump Room was open from 6 am to 7 pm except for mid-morning and mid-afternoon, and on Sundays from 6 am to 9 am and 5 to 7 pm. The Spa Hotel, where Kinellan Drive is now situated was opened a few years later and provided facilities up to the highest standards of the south. What was described as 'a comfortable inn' was also functioning close to the Pump Room. None the less there was still a great shortage of suitable accommodation for a number of years, many visitors having to content themselves with rooms in country cottages at Achterneed and elsewhere.

However Rome was not built in a day; later in the century development proceeded more rapidly. Consideration always seems to have been extended to the poorer type of patient. A Mr Gordon, an Irish Member of Parliament, opened an institution for those of limited means in 1839. Accommodation was available for fifty patients so that the building must have been fairly large. However it was not very substantial and began to fall into disrepair after a few years. Help, however, was at hand. The loss at sea in 1853 of a ship named the Pictou had attracted much attention owing to the

heroism of Dr Nicolson Mackenzie who had been responsible for several gallant rescues but himself perished in the disaster. He was a nephew of the Rev Donald Mackenzie, parish minister of Fodderty. His mother, Mrs Morrison Duncan of Naughton, Fife, thought the best memorial would be a hospital in the Spa which could meet the needs of arthritic patients not able to afford the cost of a full course of treatment. The hospital could take twenty patients and as late as the inter-war period charged only £1.0.6d per week to cover all expenses. In modern times it was taken over into the state system and is now used mainly as a physiotherapeutic unit.

The mineral wells were taken under the management of the Cromartie Estate in mid-century, and this was to prove decisive for the future. Anne Hay Mackenzie who had married the third Duke of Sutherland in 1849, became Countess of Cromartie in 1871 in her own right, having served Queen Victoria as Mistress of the Robes. She was not only a lady of considerable personal charm but also one who could convert ideas into deeds. In that same year a good stone pump room with baths was erected and gradually a complex of buildings, glass-fronted and with two towers, one pinnacled, the other square with a public clock, came into being. The Pavilion, as the impressive concert hall is called, was set in its dominant position in the public gardens with their greens for bowls, tennis and croquet, and grounds with flower beds and shady paths among the lofty trees. In the forenoon The Square bustled with visitors in holiday attire, and its central area was set around with brakes, charabancs or other conveyances, according to the period of history, offering excursions far and near. For those who preferred local jaunts the Ord Wood was laid out with paths converging on the western height with a tall flagstaff. On the southern slope of the Strath, below the Cat's Back, at the time of the Queen's Jubilee, a drive was constructed from the main road at the present youth hostel to where it linked with the road to Dingwall at Loch Ussie near the Knockfarrel summit.

About 1905 two sisters, whose cottage was nearby, set up a tent just above this junction where they provided teas with home baking for visitors arriving either on foot or by conveyance. This venture proved very successful and a few years later the Cromartie Estate built for the Misses Cameron a wooden chalet, circular in shape, with a surrounding verandah divided into bays. Wooden shutters when lowered became tables for outside guests, and allowed connection with the interior. Afternoon tea, perhaps including strawberries

76

recently gathered from an adjacent garden, enjoyed in the bracing atmosphere and spectacular scenery, was an experience very pleasant indeed.

The chalet continued in business until 1952 when it was burnt down. Three boys were seen running over the summit towards Dingwall at the time. One wonders if their consciences have ever troubled them since.

It is not so much the growth of the Spa, however, as its character which is notable. For Strathpeffer is unlike so many other places in Scotland where towns and villages have grown up haphazardly. The Spa nestles among the hills like a jewel, because its designers and developers have always insisted on the best. For this much credit must go to Anne Hay Mackenzie, who was very familiar with the continental spas. Where others had foreseen Strathpeffer becoming 'a considerable village', her sights were set much higher. Though local talent was given every encouragement, the main architects and designers were from London, and the eventual outcome, though not large in extent, is comparable with the best. The Highland Hotel, prominent though not incongruous, was not built until the first decade of this century, following the standard design of the Highland Railway. But how much better is the Ben Wyvis, reposing in its spacious grounds, now past its centenary, the result of independent imagination, initiative and good taste. Though The Square has now lost its main establishment, the remaining shops and other buildings still fit well into their setting. The visitor notices that throughout the Spa part of Strathpeffer there are not two of the larger houses alike. The same feature marks the smaller buildings too. Round about The Square there are some half-dozen constructions, all interesting and all quite different from the others. This has not happened by accident. It was planned thus and executed accordingly.

The good relationship which has always existed between the Cromartie family and the general community was made especially evident at the end of last century when the usefulness of electricity was beginning to be realised. Colonel Blunt-Mackenzie, husband of the Countess, was always interested in new developments and erected a power plant in Glensgiach, to supply the wants of the castle. But he did not limit the benefits received to his own residence, so that in a few years the cottages on the Heights and the houses and hotels in Strathpeffer were enjoying the new form of illumination and power; it was still to be many years before the majority of people in towns and cities elsewhere were to know anything better than gas. The small plant originally used became, of course, unable to cope with the increasing demand, and by 1902 a larger plant had to be installed at Loch Luichart. Eventually the enterprise passed into the hands of Scottish Power. It may be of interest to note that to ensure good work the engineer who had been reponsible for the building of the world's biggest dam was engaged to construct the Loch Luichart project. Unfortunately when a great spate arose here his Highland venture burst, and considerable repairs had to be undertaken!

The Railway

Critical to the growth of the Spa was the coming of the railway. Early last century there was a two-horse coach leaving the Spa Hotel at 8 am reaching Inverness at 11 am. Return was at 3 pm and fares 10s inside, 6s outside each way. By 1880 plans were in hand to construct what would eventually be the Kyle Railway across Ross-shire. The line was to have run from Dingwall to Strathpeffer with the station on the slopes behind the Pavilion. Thereafter it would cross the main road at the end of the Gardens and proceed by Kinellan Farm and Coul estate to Contin. Beyond, it would proceed by Rogie and emerge by Loch Garve to where the present line is laid. It can be seen how this would have opened up a wide district, which has remained isolated, and brought additional badly needed

income to the enterprise. Furthermore it would have meant that Strathpeffer itself would not have been cut off from the West Coast and would still today have had the luxury of a railway station. Unfortunately the proposal was successfully resisted by a local proprietor who, perhaps, like most of us, did not fully appreciate how much private interest may hinder public good.

Though the main Kyle line was constructed by-passing the Spa, a branch line was opened in 1885 which was for the next sixty years to play a significant part in the life of the community. During the summer months there was heavy traffic and in peak years a weekly through coach, a sleeper, from London. As trains arrived the Station Square would be lined with brakes and cabs (or, later, buses and taxis) to convey travellers to their respective destinations. But even off-season the station was an interesting place. The Strath was a commuting area for the County capital. Dingwall solicitors and other business people who resided in our more salubrious district each morning ensconced themselves luxuriously in the first-class compartments while the humbler clerks, shop assistants and Academy school-children crowded noisily and cheerfully into third. On such occasions as a distinguished visitor, an emigrating native, or a happy bridal couple were departing, fog signals would be laid on the lines as a salute. I cannot recall a time when the signals were used for their proper purpose. But then, in that clear atmosphere, I cannot remember a serious fog!

The Season
The Spa had the dignity of a season of its own, during which visitors outnumbered the natives, and had their names published weekly in the local press under their respective hostelries. Their routine set the pattern for the community. On arrival patients consulted one of the local doctors as to strength of waters and type of bath likely to be most beneficial. The Spa was open from 7.30 and the first glass of water was best consumed an hour or so before breakfast. Since the ailments of at least some were due to an over-indulgent way of life this spartan opening to the day was, no doubt, an integral part of the cure. To ensure that patrons rose in good time thoroughly aroused, a piper, in pre-war days at least, used to circumambulate the main roads and terraces in full blow from 7 o'clock onwards.

The waters were served steaming hot and giving forth a most obnoxious stench, so that one frequently saw a new arrival holding

80

his or her glass at arm's length and gasping, 'Have I got to drink this?' In due course, however, such people would be strolling about The Square or Gardens, chatting with others and enjoying sipping the beverage every moment. A second round of drinks followed at noon when music was supplied by an orchestra playing from the bandstand.

There were three main types of baths in addition to other forms of treatment. The simplest was provided by hot diluted sulphur in which one was immersed for some fifteen minutes. Absorption of the chemical into one's system often had a beneficial effect. With the *douche* one received massage on a rubber bed under a spray of heated water. But the 'piece de resistance' was the peat bath. Peat is a strongly therapeutic agent and though, of course, a variation of the continental mud bath, the Strathpeffer peat bath was the first of its kind in the world. It was a form of treatment requiring a strong heart, but if the patient was deemed suitable he was duly lowered by straps into the black morass. On emerging he found beside him a bath of ordinary water for cleansing purposes, and he could be hosed down if he wished. Thereafter he repaired to his dressing room where, covered with blankets, he relaxed on a couch until a native or a Swedish masseur arrived who subjected him to vigorous pummelling. Adjusting to out-of-doors temperatures was a gradual business necessitating emergence by inner and outer cooling rooms. This whole process, which might cost about 10s, could take up a good section of the day.

It all appeared, and was intended to be, a well organised way of life run with maximum efficiency. But 'accidents will occur in the best-regulated families' and Duncan MacPherson, who, before setting up his own pharmacy in Kyle of Lochalsh, served with T Wellwood Maxwell in Strathpeffer, tells an amusing story of an incident which occurred while he was there. A young doctor, rather contemptuous of mere druggists, arrived to take over a local practice. Among his first patients was a young lady with a skin complaint for which he prescribed a lead ointment to be applied over her whole body. Next day he recommended a sulphur bath which the patient obediently took but from which she emerged with her whole body completely black! Distraught she sent urgently for her consultant, and it was a much humbler doctor who resorted to Mr Maxwell's to seek the appropriate antidote.

At least for those of maturer years the Strath provided almost all that spa visitors could wish. For those actively inclined there is an excellent eighteen-hole golf course within ten minutes' walk from The Square.* Before 1914 there was also a shorter ladies' course in front of the Ord Wood. Walks there were in abundance in the Gardens or on the hills and what more pleasant than to saunter down to Castle Leod and watch Ross County play, say, Edinburgh Wanderers, in one of the most beautiful cricket grounds in the country? In the evening one could repair to the Pavilion where the orchestra provided a musical programme, should there not be a concert or other special event. All this speaks of a leisured way of life no longer in tune with the times. The day of the spa has faded and in all Great Britain there is now but one centre providing the full treatment here described. That there is a therapeutic value in the waters themselves can scarcely be denied since, from the most ancient times, ordinary folk have testified to benefits received. Indeed, the earliest records of Strathpeffer testify that it was the poorest section of the community who flocked from far and near, quite confident that the springs were healthful. Today drugs and local hospitals can bring treatment to hand without sufferers having to seek a distant and probably expensive spa and the old idea has gone out of fashion.

Yet though modern medicines bring instant relief in ways not dreamt of before, illness is still widespread and arthritis, the great crippler, still costs our country thirteen million working days every year. Stress is a major factor in many ailments, not least arthritis: the benefit of spa treatment lies in the fact that not only physical remedies are applied but patients have an opportunity to take life in more leisurely fashion, follow a fixed routine of life and enjoy wholesome food.

Personalities

A community so mixed was bound to have a wide variety of people associated with it. Some of the most notable figures in the social and political life of the country were among the visitors it entertained. In the garden of the only private house now standing in the grounds of the former Spa Hotel is an oak tree with a notice:

Fagus Purpurea
Planted by her Royal Highness
Princess Mary Adelaide, Duchess of Teck
and his Highness, the Duke of Teck
17th September 1895

*This, I now learn, was laid out by Colonel Blunt-Mackenzie, father of the present Earl of Cromarty, in 1902.

These were the parents of Queen Mary, grandmother of the present Queen.

Members of several European royal houses are recorded as having taken the cure at the Spa. There are those still alive who remember Ernest Shackleton's lecture on his travels in the Antarctic. He apparently had much trouble with the magic lantern by which he endeavoured to illustrate his talk, but the latter was itself so compelling as to be quite unforgettable. Duncan MacPherson also mentions a visit by Mrs Pankhurst which seems to have been anything but a peaceful occasion. In what she might have expected to be one of the most genteel gatherings in the United Kingdom she was hotly questioned from all parts of the hall and near pandemonium broke out. So debateable a question as the equality of the sexes required amazing moral and even physical courage on the part of the pioneers.

Many literary figures were associated with the Strath. The present writer has rubbed shoulders with George Bernard Shaw, sheltering under a shop canopy in The Square on a rainy day. Robert Louis Stevenson visited the district and wrote 'Near here is a valley, birchwoods, heather and a stream . . . No country, no place was ever for a moment so delightful to my soul.' Helen Keller, the blind and deaf writer, used to spend summers in a farm house in a neighbouring parish and, in different words, expressed similar sentiments. Allan Fraser spent his early years in the spa, and Neil Gunn did much of his writing in the country nearby. Particularly Strathpeffer's own was Colin MacDonald, born and reared in a croft above Achterneed station. He attained a position of responsibility in the Board of Agriculture dealing especially with Highland affairs, but was well on in life before he realised his powers as a writer of the ways of the people among whom he was reared and whom he loved so much.

Other figures of less distinction we recall and record before memory of them has gone for ever. Strathpeffer was about the last place likely to have any connection with the underworld, but I remember the occasion when the rumour went round that a guest in one of the most luxurious hotels was none other than Oscar Slater who had not long before been released from prison and indemnified after serving a long sentence for a murder in Glasgow.

There were other characters of mystery. There was for instance

Mr S, a tall, bearded rather sinister gentleman who lodged locally. He was reputed to have had sunstroke in Australia and to have been accommodated in the far north by wealthy relatives who felt embarrassed when he was too near. According to gossip he turned day into night and vice-versa and certainly only ventured out of doors in the twilight. A small boy was once said to have been beaten up by him, but this may have been richly deserved.

A popular figure was Sandy the Piper, who for an ironic reason had to discontinue the practice of stalking the streets playing Highland music to awaken the slothful: he himself became so crippled that he had to confine his activities to short strolls in front of the Pavilion. He must have done well financially posing for amateur photographers.

Belonging to a slightly earlier time, about the turn of the century, a man who had what we might today call a 'computer brain' was employed as 'boots' in one of the big hotels. He was one of those rare people who seem able to do, without conscious effort, elaborate mathematical sums almost instantaneously. Local farmers at the Dingwall auction sales who used to pose questions such as 'How many turnips in a field of so many rows and so many turnips in each?' invariably received the correct answer. The man visited a Glasgow exhibition where he entered a challenge match with an American possessing the same faculty and is said to have won a large sum of money.

Country people did their rounds frequently with eggs, rabbits etc to sell, but the most interesting arrivals would be when a bevy of fishwives from the seaboard of Easter Ross debouched from the train, be-shawled and with large black creels on their backs. As the one who usually visited us entered our kitchen she always pronounced a blessing on the house as she proceeded to the sink to gut the purchased fish. What a hard life these women had! Early in the day they set off laden to walk the five miles to Fearn station. There they took the train to Dingwall where they changed for Strathpeffer. In the spa they did their rounds, receiving at one place or another a welcome cup of tea. To save spending a penny (literally), some just stood over a street drain. Then, the creels re-filled, this time with articles required for themselves or neighbours, they made the return railway journey to Fearn and commenced the five mile trudge home. Changed days now, of course, with the fishing gone and new ways of making a living! Recently we were visiting that neighbourhood and observed a monster van bearing the family name of our own Mrs X. Possibly it is the property of her grandson, living in affluence never dreamed of by his ancestors.

The peak years for Strathpeffer were just before the First World War. At the height of the season even the big hotels would be booked out and later arrivals, however grand, had often to appeal to the owners of quite humble premises to accommodate them At the Highland Games of 1912 one of the first aeroplanes to make an appearance in the Highlands was engaged to do aerobatics over the enclosure. Never were such crowds seen in the district, nor the railway, sidings and all, so congested.

The Great Wars
The beginning of August 1914 saw Strathpeffer blistering in great summer heat. Very popular in those days were the two English picture papers, *The Daily Sketch* — now defunct — and *The Daily Mirror*, a production very different in character from what it is now. As the war clouds were darkening on the international scene, I recall the caption, possibly along the top of a front page: 'Can England keep out of it?' (Today the question might have been framed differently.) Youngsters were not unduly perturbed by the implications; the Balkan Wars had just finished and had not ruffled the surface of our peaceful existence. So it came as rather a surprise when into the room where the present writer was sitting on the evening of the Fourth came a gentleman visitor who announced very seriously, 'We are now at war with Germany!'

It might be thought that in our distant Highland resort in high summer a conflict which as far as Britain was concerned was to develop only gradually would have little immediate effect. It was not so. Visitors with naval or military commitments had to report to their bases at once, and on their departure their families also prepared to leave. Then many Highlanders were engaged in the mercantile service and their families also felt they must return home at once. So the season petered out, never in post-war years to pick up again as before.

Most young men of the district were in the Territorials, regarded as a kind of adult Boy Scouts, with activities including drilling, shooting and an annual camp. Britain had a small but efficient professional army and Territorials, as mere reservists, were not thought likely to have enough time to reach the battle-front before

the fun (as they called it) would be over. So on a certain day many of us who were then youngsters assembled on the fringes of the Station Square, mounted on fences and nearby gates, as the 'boys' gathered on the railway platform and disappeared into the waiting carriages. Envious of the lads whose adventurous destiny would be to put the Germans in their places, we gazed with wondering eyes on the mothers weeping openly and unashamed.

These 'boys' were the cream of our youth and few returned. After the war was over there arose the question of the form the memorial should take, and several suggestions were made — a monument in The Square, or a tall obelisk on Knockfarrel which would be seen far and wide. But surely the most fitting was that actually chosen, the memorial arch and gates at Fodderty churchyard — a cross on top and then the *clarsach*, or Highland harp, on which of old the bard would sing of the heroism of those fallen in battle.

Mournful remorse, however, was far from the minds of most people in Strathpeffer in August 1914. War fever descended upon us all. Rumours were rife. One-man bands and other German street musicians had been common features of our towns and villages and these were now suspected of being an army of spies. Two men of this type had been observed on the road to Dingwall and looked as if they could have had secret documents or possibly weapons on their persons. A coffin had passed through Inverness and reached Invergordon station but a vigilant station-master had been suspicious and found (it was reported) on opening it, a corpse in a good state of health!

Mysterious lights were said to flash nightly from a baronial residence where the owner was of a German family of considerable standing, and no doubt as innocent as she was cultured.

In both world wars the North of Scotland was a restricted area and all entering Inverness from the south had to present passports. One can well imagine how useful it was to military and naval commands to have such an area of land and sea coast for secret manoeuvres. The Cromarty Firth with only a narrow entrance provided what at first seemed the safest of anchorages for the British fleet, and Invergordon from being a community of 1500 inhabitants shot up to approaching 30,000. Then suddenly it was realised that the narrow entrance not only prevented the enemy from attacking but also could allow them to blockade our fleet with mines and submarines at least long enough to permit their own navy out into

the open sea to do much damage. Thus the main British fleet was transferred from Invergordon.

Then one day at the end of December 1915 we in Strathpeffer were shaken by some kind of tremor. Since military exercises were constantly proceeding in our neighbourhood, though we remarked on the occurrence, we were not unduly surprised. That night, however, we learned that the cruiser *Natal* had blown up off Invergordon with the loss of 350 lives. This was of particular sorrow to our district as a Sunday school party had been visiting the ship and all were lost. The cause of the explosion was never, so far as we know, established, but since no claim was made by the enemy it would appear to have been the result of some mishap on the ship itself. Outside our area few people were aware of the incident until after the war. The hulk of the ship was declared a war-grave, but it remained an obstruction to shipping until 1978 when it was finally rendered innocuous.

Stories, true or exaggerated, arose about the *Natal*. It was said the explosion, which rocked Cromarty, was not noticed in parts of Invergordon.

There was also a tale about some tins of TNT which had been salvaged and had been left on the shore for a short time by those in charge. When they returned it was immediately realised that one container with enough explosive to do enormous damage was missing. They dashed up to a nearby cottage to discover an old lady with it beside her and intending to open it when she had finished her cup of tea!

During both wars the hotels and guest houses were commandeered for both men's and women's services. In the Second World War The Spa Hotel, the oldest hotel in Strathpeffer, was burnt down while in use as a hospital. It was never rebuilt.

But the 1914-18 period was not of war's alarms exclusively, and at least for one growing lad it was vividly pleasurable. It is not out of place, therefore, to describe how important and enjoyable winter-time activities were in the life of the local people.

Perhaps the distance of the years lends enchantment, or a few miles north adds that touch of exhilarating severity to a Highland winter — who can say? In any case the prospect of winter brought much cheer at least to younger spirits. Behind what is now the youth hostel was the Jubilee Pond, available to the entire population for skating and curling. The great question was 'When will it bear?', and while still more than a quarter of a mile distant young hopefuls, skates draped round their shoulders, would listen keenly for the 'roaring' which would tell if curlers had begun their activities. If so, there lay ahead long hours spinning around on the ice with an occasional break to picnic on the island. For the younger fry there was also sledging through the streets. Half-a-crown (12½p) was all we paid the local carpenter for making a 'bogie'. Four pieces of wood across the two supports with a couple of lengths of piping for runners and a cord for pulling were all that was required. Then off they would go, down the Main Road and the Station Brae time after time. Of traffic there was little. If a motor vehicle appeared the event was momentous enough to warrant dismounting from one's own vehicle to make an inspection of the passer-by.

But when the American troops were with us towards the end of the First World War, how the scene was changed! To them the golf-course was a tobogganist's valhalla, and it is possible that not only a few bones but some world records were broken. But that was their own business! Not so when they came out on to the public highway, whizzing past Ulladale, down the Church Brae, round the Square and finishing up near Castle Leod! What might have happened eventually at blind crossings and elsewhere we do not know, for their authorities quickly put a stop to such adventures!

5. Post War Years — Decline and Revival

After 1945 the future of the Strath looked bleak. The spa did not reopen and with the decline in the popularity of its treatment, the main buildings, now in bad structural condition, were demolished. British Railways decided to close the Strathpeffer branch line and the rails were uplifted. One church disappeared as a church; one large hotel had been burned down and another was threatened with demolition.

Yet gradually things took a more hopeful turn. Developments in connection with hydro-electric installations and forestry created new life and brought in new population. Also it was soon apparent that the Strath, though no longer a Spa, still remained a holiday centre. The good accommodation it provided made it, after Inverness, the main resort for coaching tours in the north. During the day it might not show much activity but in the evenings with shops open and doing good business, and usually some form of popular entertainment available either out of doors or in the Pavilion, the Strath took on quite a continental air. Gradually too it began to re-assert itself in its own right. Though overshadowed by its neighbour, the District capital, Dingwall, with its administrative offices, good shops and impressive sporting facilities, the Strath maintains its own community life. The churches play an important part in this, the local golf, cricket and shinty interests are centred here, Community Council and WRI actively fulfil their functions, while the Operatic Society has for many years been a strong cultural force. Then, all visitors and residents alike can share in what the Strath has to offer of itself: exhilarating walks, breathtaking views and, on the heights, a sense of peace unsurpassed anywhere.

New times bring new possibilities. Winter is no longer the time of the dead months. The large hotels are finding an all-year-round function not only for the tourist but for local social occasions;

one of them has been an off-season school for hotel management. The derelict station buildings are to be made into a centre for arts and crafts with special concentration on Celtic and clan culture.

Various other schemes are being mooted. If, thirty years ago, the tide seemed finally out and it seemed as if the once-proud health resort was about to sink into obscurity, today the movement is in the other direction. With the industrial development in Easter Ross the Strath is recognised as one of the most desirable residential centres in the north. Nowadays there is no railway station at hand but, with the building of new, fast roads and the construction of the bridge at Kessock, Inverness Airport, with nation-wide connections, will soon be within little more than half an hour's distance. The proximity of Ben Wyvis and the hotel facilities available have consequently generated the thought that the area might be opened up for all-year-round sporting activities. Surveys have been made of the mountain as to its suitability for ski-ing and these have been very favourable. Difficulties are at present largely financial but naturally strong objection would be taken to any plans which encroached out of character with the district. There is, indeed, great potentiality in making the area a resort for mental and physical relaxation, and one hopes that a balance may be found between wise development and reasonable caution. The Strath of 1900 would have seemed strange to the natives of 1800 and it could be that the Strath of 2000 would surprise its predecessors just as much — one hopes, favourably!

Then, surprise of surprise, a movement has begun, if as yet only tentatively, to bring back to our island the day of the Spa. The suggestion has been mooted that seven spas under the National Health Service might be restored, with Strathpeffer as the centre for Scotland. When the NHS was being set up it was decided that spa treatment should be dismissed as merely trifling with serious trouble.

Indeed, such trouble is serious, since around twenty million people in the United Kingdom suffer from some form of rheumatic complaint in the year, which means not only economic loss but human frustration and pain. So the medical authorities have had reports on alternatives to the present methods in use, and greater recognition of the value of these is now being shown. For, as Dr W A R Thomson records, it is strange that in these post-war years spa treatment has flourished as never before. Britain has only one spa now in regular use — Leamington — while West Germany has 200, with over six million patients treated in 1975. Baden-Baden,

Pump Room, Strathpeffer

Allan Haldane

which Anne Hay Mackenzie knew so well and from which she took many of the ideas applied to Strathpeffer, had in 1976 half a million patients to whom the spa facilities were available under the German equivalent of our NHS. Dr Thomson notes that as far as Strathpeffer is concerned its 'virtually unique waters are simply flowing to waste', though it would take very little to convert it into a thoroughly modern spa. The Nicolson Mackenzie Memorial Hospital could well become the centre of an excellent Pump Room complex. Dingwall has a forty-bedded hospital only five miles away and Inverness its two large hospitals which could provide expert rheumatological opinion.

Some twenty-five years ago a friend of the writer's remarked that Strathpeffer could be called 'The Deserted Village'. Obviously this is not true today. We can only hope that those who come to shape its future will do so with special insight and concern. We have tried in these pages to recapture something of its long, rich and varied story. We hope that future generations will realise how fortunate they are to enjoy in their own day its woods and hills and changing skies.

BIBLIOGRAPHY

ANDERSON, George and Peter, Guide to the Highlands (John Murray, 1834).

ANDERSON, Isabel H, Inverness before Railways (A & W Mackenzie, 1885).

BAIN, Robert, History of Ross (Pefferside Press, 1899).

BARRON, Evan, The Scottish War of Independence (Rbt Carruthers, 1934).

CRUDEN, Stewart, The Scottish Castle (Nelson, 1960).

DONALDSON & MORPETH, Dictionary of Scottish History (J Donald, 1977).

FOX, Dr Fortesque, Strathpeffer Spa (H K Lewis, 1889).

GRANT, Dr I F, Highland Folk Ways (Routledge & Kegan Paul, 1961).

INVERNESS FIELD CLUB, The Hub of the Highlands (P Harris, 1975).

HENDERSON, Isabel, The Picts (Thames Hudson, 1967).

JOHNSTON, J B, Place-names of Scotland (John Murray, 1932).

MACDONALD, Colin, Echoes of the Glen (Moray Press, 1936).

MACNAB, P A, Strathpeffer Spa (Highland Lass Ltd).

McPHAIL, Rev J S, Memorials of Rev W S McDougall (Melvin Bros, 1897).

MACPHERSON, Duncan, Where I Belong (G & W Fraser, 1960).

MACRAE, Norman, The Romance of a Royal Burgh (E P Publishing House, 1923).

MELDRUM, Edward, From the Nairn to Loch Ness (Highland Herald, 1977).

MILLER, Hugh, Scenes and Legends (Various).

NICOLAISEN, W F H, Scottish Place Names (Batsford, 1976).

PREBBLE, John, The Highland Clearances (Penguin, 1963).

SUTHERLAND, Elizabeth, Revision of Alex Mackenzie's Prophecies of the Brahan Seer (Constable, 1977).

THOMSON, Dr W A R, Spas that Heal (A & C Black, 1978).

TRANTER, Nigel, The Fortified House in Scotland, V (Oliver & Boyd, 1970).

WATSON, W J, Place Names of Ross and Cromarty (Re-issued by Heritage Society, 1976).